The Soldier in You

"Life can be delusional. You'll find that you are so much stronger and more valuable than you think you are."

By Rod Cole

Cole, Rod 1965-

The Soldier in You: by Rod Cole .-1st ed.

*Summary: Life can be delusional. You'll find that you are so much **stronger**, more **successful**, and have a hidden **happiness** that you didn't know you had.*

*Have you ever been singled out and **trapped** by outside forces that you had no control of? Well, you're not alone. But you find as I have that you may not really be trapped and that the **power** has been yours all along.*

*Have you ever felt **hopeless** not knowing how you fit in this world and what you are meant to do with your life? I have also felt this way, and I'll share with you how I overcame this and discovered my **true success**.*

*Have you ever felt **oppressed** by another and could not find your own **voice** to defend yourself? You're not alone, I have as well and I'll share what I did to overcome this so as to finally realize the **strength** that I didn't know that I had all along.*

*Have you ever found that the harder that you work, the **less traction** that you seemed to make in your personal and professional life? Well, you are in a group of many that have felt just as you have. And even so, I'll help you to discover the hidden **happiness** that is within you.*

*Do you want to make a **difference** and **impact** yourself and those close to you? I want this for you also. This will take work and a shift in your **mindset**. This will require you to be a **Soldier of progress and change**. Are you ready for that? Your answer should be yes. You're ready even if you think that you are not.*

*If you answered yes to any of the questions above, don't worry. You are merely a **Soldier in the making**, waiting for your next mission. This book will help prepare you for that mission. **Read on**.*

ISBN: 978-0-9996754-0-3

ISBN: 978-0-9996754-9-6

*"I dedicate this book to my best friend and wife **Christel**, who has always been supportive and encouraging in all that I do. And to my 3 amazing kids, **Miyah**, **Ashley**, and **Ian**. As a father, I couldn't be more proud of all of you and the paths that you have chosen for yourselves."*

Table of Contents

Hello Reader. *I am excited for you that you have selected this book for your next read. My hope is that you will be truly inspired by my personal experiences along with my unique point of view. My mission within this book is to prove to you and to teach you that an unhappy life can be delusional. You'll find that you are so much stronger, more successful, and have a hidden happiness that you didn't know you had. After you finish the book, I would appreciate your feedback by rating this book.*

Thank you!

Rod Cole

Another Book by Rod Cole

Thou Son's Keeper

Fiction

ACKNOWLEDGMENTS

In life, none of us really accomplish anything by ourselves. It's usually as the result of help or encouragement from others. And I'm no different. I've had some wonderful teachers who knowingly and unknowingly helped me throughout my life. Some of my experiences have been glorious and others have been painful and disheartening. And even so, I can say with confidence that those experiences weather glorious or painful were to my benefit in lessons and overall experiences. This is why I am acknowledging all in my life that has brought me joy or pain because all were needed as my teacher at those times.

I have an amazing family that supports me in all that I do and have done. It would have been impossible to write and complete this book without the support and love of my wife Christel, and our three kids, Miyah, Ashley, and Ian.

I'm so grateful to my parents Thomas and Bernice. They have set the foundation for learning and development for our family. My mother once took me aside and said, "It's time for you to be your own man," And throughout my life, I've tried to do just that.

Most of us struggle to find mentors of some sort to help and guide us through our uncertain and challenging lives. My dad has always been this mentor for me. He has coached me through more situations than I can count. My dad and I have this saying, you never stop being a parent, and this has always been true with us.

Finally, I want to thank my two brothers Tom and Steve. I greatly appreciate their friendships and support over the years.

Thank you all.

PREFACE

"Soldiers, when committed to a task, can't compromise. Its unrelenting devotion to the standards of duty and courage, absolute loyalty to others, not letting the task go until it's been done."- **John Keegan**

I chose the tile for this book *"The Soldier in You"* not because I have a military background or experience because respectfully I have neither. I have actually never had the honor to serve in the military though many of my family members and friends have. I did not choose this tile because I'm a strong military buff that watches military strategies on the History Channel or read countless military books because I rarely do either. I've noticed that those that have served in the military either previously or currently seemed to have a unique perspective and confidence that I admire. What's even more interesting is that this shared outlook seems to transcend cultures and genders.

Four of the most admired people that I know have all served in the military at one time or another. My father served in the Army. My father-in-law, uncle, and brother-in-law served in the Air Force. All of which have either greatly influenced me and my family's lives or I have admired their unique approach to life and their successes.

This book is not about the analysis and breakdown of the soldier's psyche. Though that could be an interesting approach I am not a research writer and this is not that type of book. I'm actually relying on an observational approach that I have witnessed over the years. I titled the book "*The Soldier in You*" because the idea of a soldier is a universal concept that regardless of if we have served in the military or not we have the mutual understanding of the perceived value of a soldier and their plight. By comparison, I wanted a figure and model that would not only show the importance of your value, but I wanted to be able to demonstrate to you the similarities of your amazing life as compared to the amazing life of a soldier.

What I'm attempting to share throughout the book is that our lives are challenging. Though many of us are not and have never been in the military, we are by comparison in the battlefield of life. This arena to us can feel as dangerous and daunting as what a soldier might face in their arena of conflict. Unlike the military, we are not facing actual battle which involves life and death situations, but that doesn't change the fear and the challenges of our own situations.

I use the comparison of the soldier as a metaphor for you and myself so that we can reference back to the idea and image of a soldier as an example of how we can march forward as we face our own challenges of our own lives. I want us to have a frame of reference and mission within our hearts as we are moving through life. The idea that you are a soldier of our life can give you a commitment and understanding of your mission for yourself, your families, your communities, your country and the world. This idea of the soldier is not to be taken lightly. I find that soldiers think differently and act differently than none soldiers. We can all learn from this.

Though the book is called *"The Soldier in You,"* I only casually reference the comparison of the soldier throughout the book. The reason being I'm just looking for a mindset, a commitment to an idea for action and change. I do the comparison because I want you to have a sense of pride in who you are in your struggle of life. I want you to have a reference so that when you find yourself in a struggle you'll say to yourself that I'm a soldier, and as a soldier, this is how I'll think and act. The idea of a soldier will be a constant reminder that you have value and purpose as you move through your challenges of life.

INTRODUCTION

"Self-worth is so vital to your happiness if you don't feel good about you, it's hard to feel good about anything else." - **Sandy Hale**

Though I share some of my own personal stories throughout the book, this book is more about you than it is about me. My goal throughout these pages is to have an impact on you. Maybe you're asking yourself why I should care when really I know nothing about you. What you'll find about me is that I care about people and that one of my passions is people. I found this out by accident. For now, let's keep this about you.

Let's take a look at who you are. Take your appearance for example. What do you look like? Are you tall or short? Are you thin or overweight? Are you young or older? Are you male or female? Let's go a little deeper; what is your culture, your nationality, religious beliefs?

How about what is your educational background? Did you finish high school or even college? Maybe you're in school now. The point is I know nothing about you.

Even if you took the time to answer the questions above, I still would not know who you are. Truthfully you are so much more complicated and interesting than a few questions could narrow down. To describe who you are would take far more than just a few short paragraphs. But what I think I know about you is this; you are important and have great value in this world. The reason that I feel that I know this is because we all do. We all have value in this world. What that looks like for you I don't know, that's for you to find out as you travel through your journey. But I want to help you if you would allow me to. Keep in mind that this is not just about me helping you; this is also about you helping me. I'll explain more about that later.

For introduction's sake, I'll tell you a little bit about myself. First of all, I'm not famous. I doubt that you ever heard of me. Secondly, I don't have a lot of money. I have a stable job and make a regular living with a solid company. Most likely like you do as well. But even if you do or don't this book is not about money. This book is not about who makes the most money, and if you do this somehow makes you the most valuable. Money is important and we all need money, but this is not about money. This book is about your value to yourself and to the world.

Understanding your value is so much more important and so much more fulfilling than money. Now I say this as an assumption because I've never been rich financially. My definition of rich is if you are worth millions. That's not me at this time anyway.

I have had so many experiences that have enhanced my life and personal development that have had nothing to do with money. Oddly when I had these experiences I was sometimes chasing money and usually fell short. Some of the experiences I will share with you throughout the book. I have also made mistakes and had shortcomings that hurt my life as well. But I learned from these experiences, and it will not surprise you to know that none of which have anything to do with money.

Briefly, I'll tell you about myself, as I mentioned before because this is merely an introduction. And it would be rude for me to do otherwise. I'm 52 years old and I'm a working professional. It took me years of struggle to even get to this point. Though I like what I do I want more from my career and I believe that I can do more. I've actually always wanted to be a writer and a professional speaker like the late Zig Ziglar or Les Brown. Traveling and connecting with people or audiences appeals to me. I told you my passion is people. I've wanted to do this for many years; I just wasn't committed and didn't believe that I could pull it off. That has all changed. Not only do I think I can pull this off, I'm going for it. Hence in part why I'm writing this book. There are other reasons as well, but I'll get into that in later chapters.

This might surprise you, but I've been married for 30 years. Christel and I have 3 kids, 2 daughters, and 1 son. Long-term relationships can have its challenges and we've had plenty. We as a family have worked through all of our challenges. Because of which we are a solid close-knit family that spends a lot of time together.

Immediately I had marital problems and as a result, I went through 9 years of counseling to initially save my marriage and keep my family together, but actually ended up saving myself as well. I found out so much about myself during those 9 years. I learned that I didn't like myself and how to like myself. When the counselor said your problem is that you don't like yourself I cried like a baby. I knew in my soul that his words rang with truth for me. I wasn't aware that I didn't like myself; I just knew that I didn't feel right. But the counselor's words of acknowledgment broke through to my core, and 1 began the long journey of healing. I wanted to be a better father and husband so I was committed to this healing. Some of which I will share with you throughout the book. That was many years ago, my kids are grown now. All of which are well rounded, successful in their own right and I'm extremely proud of all of them. But I'm also proud of me and Christel for doing what we had to do to set the path for their success.

We sacrificed so much for them and ourselves including our time, finances and egos.

Most of my life I've struggled with self-esteem issues. I didn't like myself and I didn't believe in myself. And worse I was a pretender. I pretended I was confident, smart and happy when I felt the opposite. Not a good way to live. But I don't think I'm the only one. I believe there are a lot of pretenders out there. We'll get into that later as well.

I want you to know that I'm just a regular guy out there struggling probably just like you. There's nothing special about me in a sense that I'm famous or have large accomplishments. I'm hoping because of my background that I will be able to connect with others. Now in truth, as you learn from this book is that we are all special and we all have talents that we can share with the world. I must warn you it is a journey, and it can be long and hard. It will require tremendous effort, focus, and patience. And you'll need to view yourself and your situation in a different perspective than you normally do. We'll get to all that in the following chapters.

As I mentioned before this book is not about me as much as is about you and in the next few chapters we will be focusing on you. My hope is that this book will be entertaining and impactful. I name the book *"The Soldier in You"* because I believe that in life that we are soldiers. We are doing the things that we sometimes don't want to do; we are facing situations that are often very difficult. We're not only struggling with ourselves, but with others and our environment such as our jobs. We are soldiering through life facing one obstacle after another, facing one setback after another. Refusing to give up on ourselves, and sometimes others. It is a process of finding ourselves and how we fit into this life. A lot of us don't really know our capabilities and our true power. A process of not being intimidated by what life has to offer, and working hard which can be exhilarating. This is why this book is not about money. If it's your goal to make more money, I believe you will do so on whatever path that you decide to take for yourself. However, this book is not about that.

Have I caught your interest so far? I hope so. Let's give it a try. Together let's change the world. Do you know how we can change the world? We can change the world by merely changing ourselves. By changing ourselves and putting ourselves in the world as improved human beings. By doing this act we will affect all those around us.

I want to spend the next few chapters sharing and helping you to get to know you. I want you to have a glorious life. I want you to change the world, your world, your community, your family or whatever you can think of for the benefit of mankind.

I'm not a motivational speaker or even an inspirational speaker. I'm a writer, teacher, and a student. I learn and I teach. I'm a regular person with flaws just like you. I have fears to overcome and setbacks, again just like you. I wrote this book because I want to help others. But I'm also helping myself. We can help each other. I can learn from you as much as you can learn from me. Maybe you're asking what makes me think that I can help others, what are my credentials? My answer to you is that I care. And because my intent is caring I can help anyone, including you.

YOUR STORY

*"Do you wait for things to happen, or do you make them happen yourself? I believe in writing your own story."-***Charlotte Eriksson**

What is your story? As I mentioned before this book is not so much about me as it is about you. What's interesting for all of us is that we all have a story. Not only do we all have a story but we are all living a story, and this story is unraveling every minute of our lives. To a point, you have some control over the direction of your story, but along the way, so many things will happen in your life that you will not expect. Within your story, there will be moments of joy and happiness, but there will also be moments of pain and tragedy. The pain and the tragedy is the part of your life that you will not have control. A loved one passes away, a friend betrays you; a boss dismisses you and your value, you have health issues. With that said there is an aspect of your life that you will have control. You can control how you think about and view your life and your circumstances. You decide on your approach to your circumstances. When you are in a difficult situation you decide if to continue or to quit. This choice will depend on your analysis of the situation. If you're making the choice to continue, it is within your control as for how to move forward.

Who are you? Let's think about this for a moment. Take your appearance for instance. What do you look like? How tall are you? What color is your hair? How much do you weigh? Are you male or female? These are just some questions that tell me about your appearance. But does your appearance really tell me who you are? I don't think so. What about your educational background. What is the name of your high school? Or did you go to college? What kind of grades did you receive? Do you think your educational background really tells me who you are? No. Let's look at your ethnic background. What is your heritage and where are you from? If I knew your ethnic background and where you're from would that give me a good indication of who you are? I doubt it. I can make prejudgments about who I think you are based on the surface information mentioned above, but can I truly understand the depth of you from this information? Of course not. You are so much more complicated than surface information could ever tell us. As a matter of fact, we are so complex that many of us are struggling for a lifetime to understand ourselves.

What kind of questions can we ask to find out who you are? How about your name? Let's start with that. That seems very simple, why do I say this? It's an introduction. The only way to get to know people is to meet them and take the time to get to know them. You'll find as I have found that people will often surprise you. We have to move past the superficial and get to the person. You're, however, are very complicated, and as well as I try to get to know you, I cannot know you as well as you know yourself. Not even a possibility. Where we have gotten ourselves into trouble is that we allowed someone who has judged us on the superficial to convince us of their interpretation of their superficial judgments about who they think we are. Our error is that we didn't understand ourselves, nor did we make the effort to understand ourselves. So when someone came along with conviction and said this is who we are, we believe them. To avoid this you want to continually move toward understanding yourself. If you don't others can judge you on your superficial appearance and background and convince you of their interpretation of you.

As a minority male, I sometimes will come across individuals in the workplace that initially will appear to be anxious about me. This can be uncomfortable for the both of us. However, I maintain my sense of self, and in a short period of time the other person will loosen up as we get to know one another. Often we are able to transition to friends. This takes effort on both of our parts. Together we overcome our own preconceived perceptions to get to know one another. This process takes courage and an open mind on both our parts. I can't help but respect a person that is willing to take this step in a relationship. As a result, a mutually respectful friendship develops. It's unavoidable in this situation. Amazing right! Not just amazing but magical. And in a small way do you know what we did? Together, me and this person by our own efforts we changed the world. In that meeting, in that relationship, we both changed the world. We made an effort to understand one another. Together we overcame our individual discomfort and moved forward in this relationship. And even more interesting, that without one another in this interaction we would not have had this opportunity to affect one another and our worlds. It may seem trivial but it's not. This is how you change the world. One small interaction after another. You don't have to wait to have money to make this happen. You can do this act now.

We can do this to ourselves as well. We look at our own superficial representation and we'll pass judgment on ourselves as if this is all that we are and have to offer. We do this without understanding that there is so much more to us and that we can contribute. Minorities and women, in particular, will do this to themselves. There are often harmful stereotypes with black males. And because these beliefs are strong among other cultures, black males will believe these stereotypes as if it's true within themselves. This creates a psychological burden on the black male. He will put himself in a box based on his own superficial perceptions of himself. Stedman Graham the writer and speaker had referred to this box in some of his talks. A psychological prison at best. It's real and powerful. I know because in the last few years I've fought hard to keep out of this box that I had created for myself. A few years ago when I found out from a close friend that I had created this box for I cried at that moment of knowing. The tears were unexpected. But the emotional release was so powerful that it overtook my total sense of self. I was bewildered. That night I told my wife what had happened and cried again in her arms. In that day at that moment, I had found out that I was living in a self-inflicted emotional prison my entire life. This one person, a friend in that vital moment, with his piercing words, had freed me and had changed my world forever. I want this for you.

YOUR DREAM

*"Start where you are. Use what you have. Do what you can." —**Arthur Ashe***

I'm in the same situation as you. I have dreams and things that I want for myself and my family. I don't want to leave this earth knowing that I did not live up to my potential or realize my dreams. More importantly, I want to leave my family with the feeling that they can accomplish anything in the world that they desire. This creates pressure for me. Especially since the time of this writing, I will be approaching 52. Fifty-two? Where did the time go? I remember being in my twenties with dreams of writing, acting, directing or whatever. Now at 52, I have not realized any of those goals or dreams. I have to ask myself why? I can blame life and say I've been so busy trying to make a living, supporting and raising a family, that I didn't have the time. But this is an excuse and a lie that I tell myself. And even if it was true, it doesn't change the emptiness and longing that I feel for wanting something more in my life.

What's interesting about this book is that you may find that I'm different from other authors that you've come across. In other words, they can be all-knowing. This is not the case with me. I don't have all the answers, I'm not all knowing, and I'm struggling somewhat with my life. Not so much financially, but I am struggling for a purpose. And this can be a real struggle at times. But even so, I don't need to be all knowing. I don't have to have all the answers. Do you know why? I'm a student just like you. I'm learning just like you are. I don't tell you this to put myself down. I actually believe in myself, and I often love my life. I tell you this so as to be genuine with you. I know that if I'm real with you, I can connect with you. If I connect with you maybe you'll follow my words and hopefully embrace them throughout this book. That's my hope anyway. Even if you don't, yes I would be a little disappointed in myself for not being able to write in a way that captivates you, but at the same time, I must admit that I love writing this book. I love the idea of knowing that someone's world could be changed from reading this book. Having this hope and knowing gives my life purpose.

At 52 I still have dreams for my life. These are just as strong for me today as they were when I was in my twenties. I find that as we get older these dreams don't go away. That's the good news. The bad news is that over time we suppress them with our excuses, lies, and non-actions. Even so, they are still stirring beneath the surface, whispering for you to notice and take action. My dream is to write books, teach and by doing so change the world with my unique contribution that only I can provide for my world.

What is your dream for yourself? Think about this for a moment. What do you really want? This can be a daunting question and can take a lifetime to answer. Sometimes you'll follow a dream only to find out that this is not what you had wanted after all. Don't get too discouraged when this happens. This can be part of the process of dream searching. Remember that the time and effort in your dream search still counts and will lead to something else. Nothing is wasted when you are pursuing your dreams.

Not long ago I wanted to be a manager. I felt that I could make a difference as a manager of a team. I went back to school and acquired an MBA. I joined the company leadership academy which was a year-long program. I went to numerous leadership seminars. I've read just as many leadership books. I even successfully led some company projects. All of which I'm proud of. I eventually applied for leadership roles that were posted within the company. It was getting to the point that leaders of my company were taking interest and asking about my interest in upcoming leadership roles.

Along the way, after all this preparation and education I had lost interest. I was on the brink of a position that I worked so hard to obtain and I didn't want it anymore. This wasn't something that I wanted to admit to myself let alone others. But I was done. It was a long journey and I had through this journey discovered something very important about myself. I was no longer interested in the position. In fact, there was something else out there that I wanted more. It was a whisper that was calling out to me. It had been calling out to me my whole life. It took courage to make this decision, but I made it. It took just as much courage to share with others, and I did that as well. Though my dream was different, all the work that I completed previously was not wasted. It never is. All the preparation and work will continue for this other dream and help make it possible as well. It's like life knows what you're going to do in advance and prepares you for such. Even if you switch your goals or dreams, all that you've done previously is still a preparation for what you are going to do next.

So I ask again, what is your dream? Don't think in terms of what others want you to do. That will lead nowhere. Even if you accomplish the dream, it's not your dream and you won't be fulfilled. Don't just think in terms of money. The idea of money itself is usually not enough to motivate you, and to sustain you through the challenges, and the time that it may take to acquire that dream. Most likely your dream will create money for you, but the motivation is usually the dream and the money is a result of pursuing that dream. The reason why we chase money is that we are convinced that the dream is the result of the money. And that's not the case. Sometimes you'll see this with lottery winners. They'll win millions of dollars, make some large purchases, travel and at the end of a few years, they are broke and not fulfilled. The money did not make a difference in their lives. Of course, you are saying what I'm saying; I would be different if that was me. I agree you are different. You are focused on the dream and not the money. This is why your life will always have meaning regardless of how much money that you have or don't have.

Back to the question, what is your dream? I'll give you a clue. Your dream is whispering to you. It's very subtle, just beneath the subconscious. You'll have to pay attention to notice, but it's there. Once you hear and accept this whisper your life will have an immediate purpose. If you don't hear anything don't' worry. Keep listening and trying different things. Don't sit still waiting for something to happen. Get out there and experience life. The day will come when your dream will present itself and the timing will be perfect. And you'll find out that all that you've done to that point has prepared you for that dream.

Something I want you to remember. The dream that is inside of you is not a separation of you. It's a part of you, it is you. This is real. Just like when you skipped lunch and felt hunger pains in your stomach. Your body is craving and calling out for the nourishment that you had denied it. We mistakenly think that we haphazardly choose our dreams but this is not so. Our dreams are alive as our hunger is alive and they have chosen us. The reason why you know your dream is inside of you is that like hunger the dream wants you to know it's there. The dream wants you to feed it by acting on it. This is why when you are thinking about your dream just listen. It's calling to you; it wants you to know it's there.

I'll tell you a secret. The dream that is you will not judge about your educational background. The dream doesn't care if you finished high school or even went to college. It wants you to take action. It will not judge about your ethnic or cultural background. It doesn't care that you are black, white, brown or anything else. The dream won't judge if you are rich or poor. It will not judge if you are a man or a woman or even if you are young or old. Maybe you think that you have been wronged by man or that life has been unfair to you. The dream that is you will not care about any of that. The dream wants one thing from you, and that is for you to act on it, to feed it. Maybe you're thinking because of your background that it's going to be so much harder for you to accomplish your dream than for others. You could be right in your assessment of your situation. None of that matters. The dream that is you does not consider your situation. It's not hearing how difficult you think it might be. It has one purpose, and that is to continue to whisper to you for all the days of your life so that you will continually act on it. What we often misunderstand is that it's not the perceived obstacles in front of us that make us miserable in our lives. We are miserable and disheartened because we are ignoring this dream that is whispering to us, craving for us to act. When we are not acting on our dreams which are a part of us then we have disconnected from ourselves. This act of disconnection creates a feeling of discomfort and of being misplaced or lost.

This is why your dream will give you purpose, and why you must go after that dream to be fulfilled. We fool ourselves when we think that we can ignore our dreams, but since the dream is you, it's not possible to ignore. Life doesn't recognize the excuses and sometimes the lies that we tell ourselves as to why we stop at the obstacles which will cause us to avoid the dream that is us. Life doesn't acknowledge that your circumstances are often grossly unfair compared to others and that it seems impossible to even survive let alone to obtain your dream. Do you understand why? You and the dream are one in the same. That dream is you. It will always be you. Because it's yours it can't be taken away and it will not go away. Do you realize how powerful this is? It can't be taken away; it's always part of us. Your car can be taken away, you can lose your home, be fired from your job, denied a promotion, your wife can leave you, and someone can even take your shoes. But that dream that is only yours, isn't going anywhere. Just knowing this is your edge in life with your dreams. Most people don't think this way. This knowing is the motivation that will help you overcome any and every obstacle that is in your path. Remember this knowing is your edge. Because you now have knowledge about your dream there is no going back. Knowledge does that to us. It opens doors for us. Do you wonder why people around us achieve their dreams often with overwhelming obstacles? The answer is because that person and the dream are acting as one.

Though I'm asking you to think about your dreams and to even share them with me, you do want to be careful with whom you are willing to share your dreams with. Our dreams can be fragile, especially in the beginning stages when we are a little uncertain about ourselves and that dream. Like a soldier, your duty is to protect your dreams and yourself at all costs. You cannot discuss or allow the dream into enemy hands. When you allow the dream into the wrong hands by merely sharing, often that person will kill your dream and you with it. I use the word kill because this is a violent act against you and your dream. This act against you is not to be taken lightly. This harmful act could be innocently unintentional such as with a concerned parent or sibling or deliberate such as with a friend or a boss. How it comes at you doesn't matter. The results of this act are the same, death to your dream.

And really it's not that they can kill your dream because your dream will always be inside of you and cannot be killed. But they can convince you to suppress your dream and that is sad. You do it to yourself. Per the instructions of the dream killer, they talk you into walking to the end of the plank of your own accord and then they persuade you to jump. You weren't forced, they just talked you into it, convinced you that this was in your best interest. That's really how it works; you are instructed to go against yourself. Even so, I have good news. As long as you are aware of this act you can resist. As you are beginning to learn if you don't already know, you have the power. I'll repeat this. You have the power. You always have. How we get ourselves in trouble is that we were not aware that we had this power. We thought the other person had the power. We thought this way because they were the ones giving us their opinion with conviction about our dreams. The conviction could be from a place of caring or from a place of vindictiveness. Either way is just as harmful to us.

This is how powerful we are. We are not victims. This is the soldier in you. It is us that are allowing the dream killers into our lives. It is us that are allowing the dream killers to talk us out of our dreams, the dream that is you. A few years ago I learned this the hard way. A person of authority had attempted to convince me against my dream. This actually went on for a couple of years before I even realized what was happening. I was surprised and very disappointed. Not only was I disappointed in this person of authority but I was disappointed in myself. I had trusted this person, but after some time had passed my instincts had whispered to me that some of these acts were not in my best interest. Not only were the acts not in my best interest but they were actually harmful to me. Knowing this I allowed this to go on for two years. When I was finally convinced of what was going on, I took action. I disconnected from the person. I kept conversations to a minimum. At one point when my emotions were calm I confronted the person. I want you to understand something. We are responsible for ourselves. The person of authority or the dream killer is not to blame when it comes to our lives. We are to blame. We allowed it. It sounds harsh but it's true. Remember we are powerful, so powerful that we can protect ourselves or not from dream killers. I allowed this person through trust and fear to come into my life and discredit my dream. Through it all I always had a choice, I chose through fear not to make this choice. And that's on me not them.

For those of you who are doubtful that I was responsible for the situation above, let me put it this way. It's about perspective. How you are willing to look at your situations. We want to look at our situations in a way that will empower us. We are choosing to either empower ourselves or to victimize ourselves. In the example above I felt like a victim. I felt betrayed by this person of authority. Not only that, because of the position of the person I felt helpless as if there was nothing that I could do. The victim. As a soldier I allowed my dream and myself to be captured and held hostage. I allowed it. Though painful you must be able to acknowledge this. This acknowledgment gives you your power back. Once you take your power back then you can position yourself to no longer be a captive to someone else. I warn you, once you allow yourself to be captured, you may need help to get out of this emotional trap. In the situation above I was fortunate that I had help from my family and close friends.

YOUR PURPOSE

*"The purpose of life is to live it, to taste experience to the utmost, to reach out eagerly and without fear for newer and richer experience."-**Eleanor Roosevelt.***

We are all here for a reason. This is probably not new information to you. I have heard this for years. Most influential speakers and writers have expressed this. The issue then becomes do you believe it? Are you here for a reason? Does your life have a purpose? In the thick of our struggles, we doubt ourselves. At this point to even focus on your purpose, let alone take action is another dimension of effort and time that we may not be willing to take on at that time. Instinctively we understand this but as a result, we still choose to avoid our purpose.

What's interesting is that your purpose is not like your dream though it can be viewed as such. Your dream is 1 or 2 ideas that you aspire to accomplish that can take a lifetime. The dream though it is a part of you is a deliberate act toward something. You must take action and have a specific mindset for it to happen. Your purpose is your mere existence and all that you do or don't do in your life. Your purpose can not be defined, it just is. Your purpose is unlimited. You cannot even measure or even understand the depth of its existence. Even after you are gone your purpose can exist for generations to come.

Our dream serves us and is meant only for us. Though it can serve others in some capacity it is still yours to share with the world or not. My dream is that I want to write books and teach. This dream is somewhere in the future. Not quite here yet, somewhere in time which is what makes this a dream. Your purpose, on the other hand, is you serving or affecting others by your existence. This is an act that has already happened and we may or may not understand what the actual act is, the meaning of the act or even how it may have helped or affected others. It's history. Once you close the gap on time and achieving the dream, then it becomes your purpose, it was something that you were meant to do and now it's part of your existence. It's your history.

Whatever you are doing today or have done at a specific time is your purpose at that moment. For example, I'm writing this book at this moment at 4 AM in the morning. This act becomes part of my history and therefore becomes my purpose. My purpose is my existence. I can also say that because I have been married for 30 years and have had 3 kids that my purpose was to be married 30 years and to have 3 kids. I've done it or I'm doing it so this has to be my purpose. My dream for the future is still to write books and to teach, but my purpose is what I've already done and what I'm doing at this moment. Now one day my hope is that my dream becomes my purpose as it becomes part of my history. The point is your life is purposeful every minute of every day. Regardless of what you do your life has purpose and meaning. We just don't take notice and as a result, many of us don't understand our value in our worlds. For me, this view of your purpose is the most exciting and is usually overlooked. This approach will give your life immediate value and direction for your purpose.

Let's look at Michael Jordan the retired basketball player. In retrospect, we can say that he was a basketball superstar and that his purpose was to win 6 championship titles throughout his impressive career. Because this is now well-known information and a part of his history, we can now say that this was his purpose. However, before Michael Jordan acquired his championship titles this thought of winning 1 championship let alone 6 was merely a dream for him.

There is another way to view our purpose, and this approach is an immediate knowing of our purpose. This way of looking at your purpose lets' us know that we have value every moment of the day. This is critical because so many of us don't understand our value. And when we don't understand our value, we may be convinced by ourselves or others that we cannot obtain a goal or a dream. That we cannot step forward and take our place in the world. Worse we may grow to not like ourselves and that would be a tragedy. There is no reason for you not to like yourself, none. Yet many of us stumble through our lives convinced otherwise. This thought process can offset your whole life and rob you of your potential to impact yourself and the world.

Every act that you do in your life is you living out your purpose on a small level. This morning when you yawned, opened your eyes and reached for the alarm clock was you living out your purpose. It's really that small of a step in your life. Then you pulled back the blankets and stepped out of bed. A small step but yet another purpose that you fulfilled. You stumbled across the room and washed your face. Do I need to say it? Yes, all that involved your purpose. Why? Because you did it, it was action, though unconscious and now it's part of your history. Then you did a whole serious of steps to brushing your teeth, taking a shower, getting dressed and now you are at your breakfast table eating your eggs that you made. This was all a part of your purpose, every single act that leads up to finally eating your eggs. This is just the first hour of your day; however, the whole day is like this. One purposeful moment after another. An endless number of acts throughout the day. This goes on day after day, week after week, month after month and year after year until finally, you have completed a lifetime of purposeful acts.

This may seem silly to look at your purpose in such a small way, but it's not. When you think about your day you accomplish so many acts that you don't give yourself credit for. We actually take it for granted. Getting out of bed takes effort and you did it. Maybe you're saying you didn't have a choice, you had to go to school or work, but it doesn't matter, you still did it, hence you served your purpose. Even if you chose to stay in bed and skip school, or call in sick to work, you are still serving your purpose. Why? Because you chose not to get out of bed, which is an action, and this choice is now a part of your history.

Having the perspective of your purpose in this way gives you some control and direction of your life which gives your life meaning. Since you know that waking up and getting out of bed is your purpose, you can decide to get up 10 minutes earlier so that you have a little more time relaxing at breakfast before you start your hectic day. You changed your purpose so that your day starts out more relaxed. If your day is more relaxed then this may change how you interact with your co-workers. A relaxed and energized you may create a different experience throughout your day. This was created by tweaking your purpose of when you get up in the morning that could change your whole day. A small example, but I want you to understand that you can have control over your purpose on this level.

We can expand our purpose. At one point I was 224 pounds. At 6 foot this was a little overweight. At 224 pounds was I living my purpose? The answer is yes. This was my existence and history at that time. I may not have liked the results, but this was still my purpose. I did have a goal or dream for myself which was to get down to 205 pounds. To accomplish this goal I had to change my purpose each day. Before I didn't monitor my calories and ate whatever I wanted. I also regularly stuffed myself. Thought I had to eat everything on my plate, and get seconds and eat all that as well. I often ate out including fast food which I love. Even so, I made those choices above and all was within my purpose which also caused my weight to climb to 224 pounds. Therefore weighing 224 pounds was my purpose. I did this to myself.

So what did I do to lose 19 pounds? I changed my purpose. I cut and monitored my calories daily. I stopped eating out as much, especially fast foods, and I joined a gym and worked out at least 3 days per week. I was conscious and had control of my purpose every day. Within a few months, I had lost 19 pounds and was down to 205 pounds. I'm still living my new found purpose because I'm still at 205 pounds. However, I have a new goal of my weight. I want to get down to 200 pounds. To accomplish this I'll need to adjust my daily purpose so that I can reach this goal. This may seem trivial, but the point is to be aware of your purpose so that you steer your life in the direction that you want.

Let's look at the bigger picture and how it relates to your purpose. As I mentioned before my dream is to write books and teach. Is this my purpose? Not yet but it could be. The reason why is because I have not accomplished this yet, it's not part of my present or history. Once this dream becomes a part of my present or history then it is my purpose. That being said I want to steer myself toward that dream. And this will be accomplished by my daily, weekly, monthly and yearly purpose. For me to accomplish my goal I need to be aware of the purposeful action that relates to that goal. Throughout our day we are living an unlimited number of our purposes such as getting out of bed, brushing your teeth, the clothes that you choose to wear, your interaction with people, your performance at work and on and on. It's endless and you choose what to focus on. Within your busy day decide on a purpose that you want to focus on that will affect your long-term dream that could turn into your long-term purpose. Let's take my dream of writing a book. How do I go from never to have written a book to writing a book?

Over the years I've taken many deliberate purposeful steps to get to the point that I can write a book. These steps were implemented in my daily life. To do this I consciously created purposeful steps that directed me toward my dream. Keep in mind that every act that we do in our lives will create our purpose. This is usually unconsciously guided by our beliefs about ourselves. We are just not aware that we are living and creating our own purpose with or without our acknowledgment. That being said the power to guide our purpose for ourselves must be a choice. So if you want to move toward your dream you must add purposeful steps in your life that will direct you toward that dream. If my dream is to write a book but I have never written a book, then I will need to add the purposeful steps of learning how to write a book in my daily life. Some of the purposeful steps that I could implement in my life are to buy books from authors on how to write books. I could take a writing class at a local community college. I could check out books about how to write books at the local library. I could study interviews with authors and learn about their writing process. I could even buy and read books from several authors to learn their various styles of writing. This list is endless of what I can do to start the process of learning about writing books. The point of this is that I'm moving from the unconscious to the conscious and in a deliberate act to take control of my purpose and guide it in the direction of my dream. It's that simple. Be aware of your dream and add purposeful steps through your day that will guide you toward that dream.

If this is your dream that is you then you will be excited about planning and implementing those purposeful steps into your life. You'll actually become energized in anticipation of the planning and work that will be required of you. Your life will instantly become an adventure that you will enjoy and look forward to. If you, however, feel overwhelmed and dread of what you may have to do within your daily purpose, then this may not actually be a dream of yours or part of you. If you find that you hate every moment as you move toward that dream, and only the end result is of interest to you then this could be just a wish. As we mentioned before your dream is calling to you and does not care about your educational background or your experience. The reason for this is because your purpose that is guided by you will align itself with your dream. If you don't have the experience to move toward that dream, your purpose per your instructions will be to get that experience throughout your life. The act of planning and implementing this experience into your life will feed that dream. This is also the same with your educational background. If your dream requires from you to have education or knowledge, then your purpose with your direction will seek out this education or knowledge. This education could be going back to school or college. Of course, this is not the only way. You may seek knowledge that you need in other ways. My wife supported our family for years and has had an amazing career in the corporate world. She accomplished this year after year without a college degree. Do you know how she did it? She educated herself. Whatever she felt that she needed or wanted to learn, she would either take a class, buy the book or ask for help. She continually trained and taught herself what she needed to know to obtain her dreams. Our house is full of books and training material that she has bought over the years. Though she was not in a position at that time to get a full degree, she still through her purpose directed herself to take the steps to educate herself, so as she could feed her dream. This act had paid off tremendously in her career.

Why does all this even matter to you? Understanding your purpose in this way will help you to understand and appreciate your value. As a soldier, you must fortify yourself. This is initially created by understanding your value to yourself and your world. This value of yours is created every moment of each day as you realize one purposeful moment after another. This understanding will help you to defend against those that misunderstand your value with their superficial interpretation of who they think you are, and try to convince you otherwise. As a soldier, you must always work toward understanding your value. This is why it is crucial to appreciate your daily purpose.

I learned this the hard way and I'm still paying for it. I had a manager continually tell me that I was not good enough, and I believed them. Why did I believe this person? I was not fortified nor did I understand my value. As a result, when this person of authority had attempted to convince me that I was not good enough I actually believed them because I did not have a basis for my own belief. In essence, I allowed this to happen. As a soldier, I'm responsible for myself and my actions. Remember I'm not a victim and neither are you. From this experience, I learned a very powerful lesson which I'm passing on to you with this book. Some of us lie to ourselves thinking and acting as if our lives don't have meaning or value, but the truth is your life has an endless stream of meaning and value. Because your consciousness and awareness were once closed you just didn't give yourself the acknowledgment for it. Now you and I know different. As result of this knowing our worlds have instantly changed.

WHY ARE WE REALLY HERE

*"Create. Not for the money. Not for the fame. Not for the recognition. But for the pure joy of creating something and sharing it."-**Ernest Barbaric***

Yes, we are here to live our purpose and to explore and connect with our dreams. But there is another reason why we are here. This reason is more subtle and not so obvious. I learned this from the late speaker and teacher Earl Nightingale. We are all here to be of service to one another. In just about everything that we do, we are using and providing service to one another. I'll share some examples of how others have provided a service to you in your daily life. These minor examples won't solve your problems in life, and won't make your journey for going after your dreams any easier, but you may afterward have an appreciation for the contribution of your fellow man.

Let's start with your bed. Where did it come from? Who invented it? Who manufactured it? What retail store offered it for sale to the public? Who sold it to you? Who delivered it to your house? In short, you have the luxury of waking up in a bed every morning because others have provided a service so that you could do so. All the questions above are an indication of a service that is being provided for that one product, the bed. You can ask these questions about everything that you see and own.

How about the indoor toilet in your home? We know that there was a time when an indoor toilet was not even available in the home. The bathroom facilities were either an outhouse that was several yards away from the residence, or at the minimum, in the residence was a bowl of some sort that was for your bathroom usage in the middle of the night. By today's standards can you even imagine the inconvenience existing in such a situation? Because the majority of us have never had to go without an indoor toilet, we take it for granted how the idea of the indoor toilet provides a service to us every day of our lives. The indoor toilet was actually invented in 1596 by Sir John Harington. However, the indoor toilet did not catch on until the 19th century. Amazingly enough, your life is actually being affected and improved by a person who lived hundreds of years before you just from this one invention.

Look around, how else do you see that you have been provided a service by others through products. Your list should be endless. Just in my office alone, I can probably list nearly a hundred ways that I've been serviced by others through products. Items that I see are my desk, my chair, the computer, keyboard, computer screen, paint on my walls, my bookshelf, stapler, calculator, pens and on and on and on. These items though I have taken for granted, have enhanced my life along with others.

In the above mentioned how we receive service from others via products and inventions. There, however, is another aspect of service which is from the direct service of others. Most of us fit into this category. I once walked into my favorite fast food restaurant. When I approached the counter, the young man standing at the register just looked at me. He didn't say a word. I was a little stunned for I did not receive the customary greeting that I was accustomed to as a customer. I looked at him, he looked at me. This went on for a few seconds. Oddly, I think I was the only one of the two of us that had actually felt uncomfortable in this situation. I said hello to him. He said nothing. I finally looked up at the menu behind him searching for the items that I wanted to order. I asked the young man for the price of one of the items. He shrugged his shoulders. He just didn't care. This young man was in a position to provide service to another. He did the bare minimum. This act of poor service affected my experience. So much so, that I never went back to that location.

Through our work, we are in a position to provide service and create value in each other's lives. This is how we can change the world and make a difference in a small way. That young man in that fast food restaurant was rude. His attempt at service was poor at best. I don't believe he understood are or even cared about the value of his role and how his actions could affect people let alone the business. He was there to collect his paycheck and nothing else. To himself, his act of service to others was of a minimum effect. However, his actions were powerful which made him influential. He caused me to feel uncomfortable and a little upset, which affected my experience while ordering my lunch. We all have this power of influence through our interactions and service to one another. The key is to understand the value of our service that we are sharing with one another.

We make the mistake of downplaying our own value of service that we can provide to others because of the type of job that we are doing at that time. In the fast food industry there about 152,000 fast food restaurants nationwide, that employed approximately 3.7 million people. This is a 208 billion dollar industry per year. That young man with the poor service is part of this amazing industry that so many of us enjoy. He didn't understand his value of his contribution to this industry and the public as a whole.

With him and millions of others like him, this industry could not be supported or exists. Therefore his value as a whole is huge.

This is just in the fast food industry. How about the industry that you currently work in? Do you understand your value of service to one another as it relates to your customers, co-workers and yourself? How is your industry, your company and you contributing to the service of man? We look at our work and we say to ourselves that we are doing this to earn a living, but there is so much more to our work than that. Our work was created so that we can serve one another. That being the case, this means that all of our work has value.

I currently work in the insurance industry. The company that I work for provides insurance protection for nearly 60,000 businesses in my state alone. They are dominating the market. I've seen firsthand the value of service that has been provided to our customers over and over again. I've seen the commitment to community involvement of this company and how their efforts have affected those that are in need. Not to mention how we are encouraged by the company values to support one another in our work. This expectation of effort and support to one another has created a unique corporate culture. We at this company understand our value to one another to the customer and the public as a whole. Through our collective efforts, we are attempting to change the world in this industry. As result of this corporate culture, we as employees instinctively understand the significance of our contribution as a whole, not only to one another but also to the customer and the public.

Sadly this is not the case with many other companies that are out there. I know because I've worked in a few. In many companies, you don't feel like you are a part of anything significant. We are basically just working for our paychecks and we are silently miserable every minute of the day. Like our fast food friend in the example above, we are not motivated to provide an elevated level of service to the customers, co-workers and one another. This type of environment is not supportive of your true value of service and what you are meant to do in this world which is to serve one another. Though the damage may not be as obvious as our friend in the fast food restaurant, we are still hurting one another from our lack of understanding of our value as it relates to providing service to one another. It's this lack of understanding and unawareness that can be so frustrating to employees. We instinctively underrate our value and purpose, though we will not express or communicate so. This type of environment can stagnate everything that we are in this world. As a result, we are miserable. Oppressed within a system that is unaware of our circumstance and yet powerful enough to affect our existence.

We sometimes hear about the companies that talk robustly about providing good service to their customers. They have a process in place for their customer-oriented approach. There's sometimes a training program in place for their staff. Customer satisfaction is strictly monitored and measured through frequent surveys. Disciplinary action is often taken for employees that mismanaged conflicts with upset customers. With all that is mentioned above, there is something very important that is missing here. Do you know what it is? It's the lack of perception that the employee is also a customer to the business that is missing here. In the situation above the employee's contribution and value is overlooked. Though the business can have a strong focus on their customer base, in the process they seemed to have very little focus on their employees. They merely have demands on the employees but not making an effort for the employees. Is as if the employer is saying I gave you a job and that should be enough. But the job itself is never enough. Employers should put the same amount of effort in the employees as they do the customer base. The reason for this is twofold. Their employees are usually the face of the company and have the contact with the customer. If the employees are genuinely taken care of they will almost effortlessly take care of the customer with their unique approach. We as customers love when someone serves us that seem to want to take care of us in their unique way. Though helpful it can be annoying when some serve us with a canned approach and seem not to be genuine.

Starbucks is a great example of the unique individual service that their employees provide to their loyal customer base. These employees are initially put through an extensive training program, partly online. Afterwards, they seemed to have an individualized approach to the service that they provide. They come across as very genuine. The philosophy of Howard Schultz the CEO of Starbucks is that the employee is first and the customer is second. When I first heard this a few years back this seemed backward to me. The philosophy has proven to be a genius approach for this organization. Howard Schultz believes that if his business makes the employees their first priority in regards to benefits, competitive salary, training and fair treatment, then his employees in return will take care of their customer base. As of the year 2016, Starbucks has had a total of 13,172 retail stores in the US alone.

Starbucks is very public about their corporate values on how they treat and value their employees. I find that when the public is aware of this type of value system, they will pay more to participate and support such a structure. My wife and I will often shop at Starbucks, but not just because the coffee is good though it is very good, and not just because the service is good, and that the environment is inviting. All true as well. I genuinely shop at Starbucks to support and be a part of a unique system that values and supports its employees. When I buy my coffee I feel good knowing that the person that served me is valued and treated well.

Companies are understandably concerned about their bottom line, but unfortunately, they will often give in to the pressure and take shortcuts with their most valuable resource, their employees. This approach can create discontent within the workforce. Though they will most likely not express their feelings to the leadership for fear of retribution, they will chatter among themselves. The workers are aware of everything that is done for their benefit or not as an indication of their value with their employer. Their overall morale will drop when they don't feel valued or protected by their employer who is in return asking and sometimes demanding so much of them. The relationship should be mutual, but because of the power of the employer, it can become one-sided. This can be frustrating to a member of a staff that wants to provide meaningful service and make a difference. This type of system can exist because employees want and need jobs to support themselves and their families. Some companies knowingly or unknowingly will take advantage and expose this need. Either way, this will create damage to the customer base, the employees, and the business.

Our lives can be structured in a way that does not value or appreciates our daily contributions to share our service to one another. Because of which we ignore the numerous opportunities to do so. What we do is we get caught up in the culture of our environments whether at home, in public or at work that will dictate to us that our acts of service are not appreciated or in the worst case scenario not even wanted. This type of situation over a long period of time can cause us to devalue ourselves. We forget who we are and our value. We actually learn and believe in this environment that we are not valuable. When people treat you as such for a period of time, as a human being who is adjusting to your environment for the mere reason for survival, you can't help but believe them. But this is a lie that you not only tell yourself but you also believe.

Why is this information important? Our most basic need and the reason why we are here is to serve one another. As a soldier that wants to contribute through your service, you must be aware of the terrain and your value within this environment. Regardless of the hazards, the soldier is certain and unyielding of the contribution that they will make in their situations. We are here to serve one another. This knowing within us will not change because of our circumstances. Regardless of your environment or obstacles, find a way to enjoy the services that are provided to you every moment of your life, and fight to present your best service to your world. Even when you are not supported your service is needed and will have an impact with those that you interact. This is how you will impact and change your world. More importantly, this is how you will fulfill yourself.

BACK TO YOUR STORY

*"The whole story is about you. You are the main character."- **Don Miguel Ruiz***

Let's gets back to you. Who are you, what is your story, how did you get here, and where are you going? I bet you have an interesting story to tell about yourself. How do I know this? Everyone has an interesting story to tell about their abundant experiences. Stories, that because it's us, we will often discount them as no value.

Your purpose doesn't necessarily need to be something grand, such as discover the cure for cancer, though that could be you. Maybe it's for self-discovery; maybe it's to invent or create something to enhance mankind. Maybe you are here to start a business, to hire employees and to enrich people's lives. Maybe you are here just to be a good father.

What is your story and how did you get here? Think about it for a moment. Where were you born, and what happened after that? What were the experiences that you've had? What was your favorite part of growing up? What brought you the most pain? What's your story? What are the significant moments in your life? One of mine is when some kids said I was ugly and I believed them all my young life. This created a low self-worth for me. Something that I still fight to this day, even as an adult. What about you? What's a life-changing event in your life that you had to overcome, or maybe you have not yet overcome it yet? Just think, let's find out who you are, and how did you get here? If I asked you to tell me about your life what would you say? Keep in mind I'm not asking for you to tell me about yourself. As important as you are, I don't want to know that yet. I want you to tell me about your life, like a movie. The beginning the middle and now. I want to know. Why, because I know you are fascinating and you have a fascinating story to tell. You know it's true. Think about it for a minute. If you have time write it down. You may be surprised. Have you ever told anybody your story? The reason that I ask is that most of us are pretenders. When people see us, all they can see is what we let them see. The superficial smile, the bright new clothes, the fancy car. Whatever I want you to see. My perfect little life as I pretend and share with you and others. Boring and unexciting. Your real story is hiding beneath the surface afraid to come out. Maybe even ashamed. I've been there, and I still have parts of me that I don't want to share. But not all of me.

You see your story is so much more important than the anything that you can make up. You as a person are so unique and so much more interesting than you can make up. We try to portray ourselves as flawless or with some perfection. We think that we as a perfect person make us more valuable to others and ourselves. It doesn't. I'll say it again, it doesn't. We know you're not perfect. We know you are not that good. Though you may try to be good and move to perfection which can be admirable, we still know that you are not perfect. You are not that good. When you try to create this perception of being someone that you are not, this creates an invisible wall between you and who you are trying to impress. This deception creates an immediate disconnect. The disconnect occurs for two reasons. First I don't know about you but I cannot connect to a perfect person. The key word is connected. I can talk with a perfect person, I can maybe interact with a self-proclaimed perfect person, and I can communicate superficially with this type of person. You know talk about the weather maybe sports if I cared about sports, or even discuss a good movie. But it ends there. I would not be able to connect as one human to another. If I had something of value to share I could not share this information with a pretender. And what's interesting I may not have an understanding of why I'm not able to connect with a pretender, but it just feels like I can't.

And then how does this interaction make the pretender feel? The pretender is not necessarily a bad person or even dishonest. They are afraid to present themselves because they may think to do so may get them excluded or even have judgment passed on to them. So they play it as they see it in their mind as safe. And they pretend that they are perfect.

There is a huge drawback to this. First pretending is a lot of work, and there is constant fear that you will be found out. I know because I've been a pretender for many years. And then when does the pretender show up? You are in and out of character. One minute you are you, the real you, the next minute you switch to the pretender. As the pretender, you are constantly gauging people's reactions to you. It's like being a performer on stage like an actor; you want to know how people are reacting to your show. Do I keep the show going or do I change up for my audience? It's sad. Even as I write this I feel pain and embarrassed. I don't really want you to know this about me. But this is the only way I can prove to you that we are a lot alike. This is one of the ways as I mentioned to you in the earlier pages that I'm going to change the world. Well, I'm not going to be able to change the world as a pretender. I'm not going to be able to help you if I'm not honest. But it's not just about honesty. It's about connection. If you see what I'm going through or see what I have been through, then perhaps you will trust me and read on. Now as you read this, know that I don't have all the answers. Not sure anybody does. But maybe you can learn from my life and mistakes, or maybe reading my thoughts will encourage you to have thoughts of your own which might be agreeable or disagreeable from my thoughts. Either way, the goal I hope is the same. Let's make not just our lives better but the lives of our loved ones and friends and the world better because we are in it.

There is also the other side of the spectrum. The person that pretends that they are not as capable so that they fit in. You know, we don't want to make anyone feel uncomfortable around us, so we downplay ourselves. We pretend that we are not as good as we maybe are so that we somehow fit in. At least that's what we tell ourselves. We don't compete as hard because if we win, then someone might get upset with us, and then there we are not fitting into the group. So that what's we think anyway. Again I've done this. It's a stupid thing to do. I've once made this decision with a job. I didn't apply for a job because someone that I knew was applying. And then that person got the job. I didn't feel better because the person got the job, I felt worse. I was upset with myself for not trying. Maybe you've done the same, I hope not. But my point is I may not be any different from you, or you may find that you would never have done some of the things that I have done. That's ok too. The point is that I'm sharing with you. Or you are sharing with me. Not so that I can hear you, but you're thinking right now. You're thinking because of what I have written.

So tell me your story, in your thoughts let's hear what you have to say. It's just me and you. Stop reading or listing to this audio and talk or think. Think about your life. Where are you in your life? Are you happy or sad, or maybe you are not sure? What happened to you today? What's going on in your life and how are you dealing with it? Why do you think you are living the life that you are? Whether you are happy or sad or just existing how did you get there? Are you looking to do something different? If so how do you plan to do it?

You know what's amazing about you and me? Is that there are lots of books out there to help us get through life and possibly to thrive and to reach our goals. And there is probably something in every book that can help us, but truthfully, deep down we already know what we need to do to be successful. We know what we need to do to make our lives work. You know what the problem is? We don't want to do it. We already know it's going to be hard. We already know that we have a lot of growing and learning to do. We already know that we could be months or years away from what we want. And that can be very daunting to us. Knowing that if I work my ass off today and do everything that I know I should do, that I still won't reach what I want until much later. Not only that, but to reach what I want, I would have to work this hard consistently day in and day out just to reach what I want in the far distance. Knowing that and anticipating the sacrifice that we will need to make is overwhelming. So we do nothing for a while. We procrastinate.

Now that you thought for a little while about yourself and your story. You probably didn't sit long, but in the time that you sat what do you think about your story? Separate yourself for now and just think about the story. If it weren't your story and you were watching someone else's story what would you think? Would you find it sad, or happy, or horrific? How about exciting? Your life is exciting. Not like the movies with all the explosions and gunfire, though it could be that way. How about when you saw Jennifer when you were 17 years old and you somehow got the nerve to go ask her on a date. And what did she say? Did she accept or not accept? It doesn't matter, it just that the experience was amazing. If she said no, what did you do after that? Did you avoid her, and then when you came around the corner you ran into her and accidentally knocked her books on the ground? Did she curse you and pick up her books? Again it doesn't matter, it's just an adventure.

You see what I mean. Your life is interesting. The more you think about it the more you'll realize how interesting you and your life are. Again this is not the movies, though I like movies. This is real with real danger and real excitement and real fears and real pain. And you have lived it all. And you are living it. See how this is not just about money. How this is so much more full filling than money. Just money alone is empty. Don't get me wrong I understand we need money, and I want money. But this is about your search and my search of self. So do you see now why this is about you because it is about you?

Do you see now how important that you are? And this is not about how successful you are. This is not about how much money you have, though I want you to have money. This is about understanding how important your life is. It's about you understanding the value of your journey and what this means to you. It's not about living a perfect life and that if you don't live up to this perfection that your life doesn't have value compared to someone else's life. It's not about that for anyone. This is about your story. Let's say your story has been that for the last 6 months you have been living in your car. Wow! How did you get there? What is your story and how you got to that point? I'm sure it's painful and sad to you but there's an amazing story there for you. And you know what else? There is an amazing story and how you are going to pull through. Do you see what I mean, you're living this story, you're living this amazing life, and you are figuring this all out like the rest of us. And we all have choices though we don't think that we do. So we feel stuck in the present situation because we don't believe that we have a choice in our current situation. But you do have a choice. You just need to think about it. These choices in front of you with all your emotions and history are what make your life so interesting. If you didn't have the baggage of your past and all those emotions, I'm thinking your life would probably be dull and not worthwhile.

I can't say enough about how important your life, journey and your story are. Once you have an understanding that no matter what is going on in your life, that you have this tremendous value, that you are so important not only to yourself but to the world. You will then move forward with an understanding that your life has real value and meaning. The problem is we forget who we are and because of which we don't have an idea of our value. This is why looking back on your life as if a story is huge. We are so caught up in our daily struggles that it never crosses our minds that we are the lead character in our lives. And that everything around us is for us and about us. Even your hardships and struggles.

So the first step is to understand your value. And that's why I want you to look at your story and like a good movie or good book, and really appreciate it. Root for yourself, laugh at yourself and cry if you must. But know one thing. You are going to win. Yes, you are going to win. And why are you going to win? Because it's your story, and you are the writer, and you have decided that you are going to win. It's that simple. It's just a decision. One that you need to make for your story. You are going to win. You'll come out of this ok. You will overcome all the obstacles and setbacks. You will decide to keep moving forward though it seems impossible. Why?

Because this is your story, and you will decide through your thought process and choices how it ends. And you know what? Others that are watching will be influenced by you and your story. And do know what they'll do? They will create their own amazing stories. And then do know what you've done? You've just changed the world for yourself and for those who were influenced by you.

We often look at our current or prior circumstances and we judge and label ourselves by these circumstances. Some of us were born in poverty or live in poverty. Others were raised by a single parent and struggled financially because our fathers walked out. Some of us have been abused emotionally or physically. Others have people in their lives that don't value them or their contributions which can contribute to low self-esteem. I'm no different. My circumstance was the prison that I created for myself as a black male. I felt obligated to conduct myself in a way so that others would feel comfortable, would not be threatened and in some cases would not fear me.

Let me tell you a secret. Our circumstances that we have lived and experienced are not necessarily who we are. I admit this can be difficult to comprehend. There is a powerful physiological and emotional connection to your circumstances and environment that makes it extremely difficult to create a separation of you from these conditions. Even so, I believe your circumstances are not intended to represent who you are, but instead are meant to be your arena for teaching moments so that you can maneuver yourself toward your dream, through those combat situations, to strengthen you in all the areas that life needs to prepare you for, in all that you are going to do. Your combat situations can be times when you are facing fear, choosing courage or fighting for something. That arena that you were born in or currently live in is needed for your growth. All of our arenas are different and personalized for us. This is why your challenges and experience are unique to you than for others. Though you may be in an arena of poverty, you are not the poverty. Though you may be in the arena where others discount your value, you are not a person of low value. I believe these areas are catered specifically for your growth and development.

Because of the challenges of our lives, we think because our father left us, that we are somehow being punished, and that we now have fewer opportunities than others that may not share the same experience. Not necessarily true. Yes, your life is difficult and challenging, and it may be more so than others. None of that matters. Keep in mind that this arena that you live and experience is unique and specifically structured for you and your benefit only. This is your arena of your life. Pay attention to it. Figure out how to maneuver through your arena toward your dreams. All that you will need to learn and experience so that you can change the world with your purpose and dreams will be gained from your experience in that arena. Often your arena will not seem fair. Do you know why? Because it's not fair. In the U.S its citizens and government had contributed to developing the Civil Rights Act of 1964, which in part is to provide equal protection of laws and policies regardless of sex, race, color, creed, or national origin. As a great nation, we have evolved tremendously over the years under this Act. And of course, we'll get even better over the next generations to come. With that being said you must understand that your arena of experiences of teaching and combat regardless of who you are does not function with the idea of equality. It is not to be compared to another's arena and experiences. Your arena is unique and specific only to you as others arenas are unique and specific only to them.

The late Nelson Mandela the once human rights activist, served 27 years in prison only to come out to be the President of South Africa. Not only that he was one of the most admired and influential men of the world. Was it fair that he spent all this time in prison? Fair or not, his arena of experience contributed to the amazing leader that we all admired. Candy Lightner the founder of the organization Mothers Against Drunk Driving (MADD) was created at out of her arena of pain and loss because her 13-year-old daughter who was a pedestrian was killed by a hit and run drunk driver in 1980. As a result of this tragedy, she created national attention and awareness about the harmful effects of intoxicated drivers. To this day deaths because of drunk driving is down 50%. Is it fair that she lost her daughter to such an act? Most of us have not experienced such a loss.

I have my own arena of challenges that I have faced throughout my life. But I have many times thanked God for my amazing life and for the very circumstances that have prepared me for my purpose and dreams. I feel in part that I was born as I am with all the experiences that came as being who I am to teach and to prepare me for my purpose and dreams that are calling out to me. This arena though imperfect is perfect for me. This is why looking at your story is so important. When you find as I have that though you are not perfect and your circumstances are even less perfect, your arena of your life and why you exist is in perfect harmony with your purpose and dreams. This realization is so freeing. Do you know what we do? We are watching others and expecting our lives to be like theirs. That's not going to happen. Your life is not meant to be like theirs. Your life is only meant to be like yours. That is an amazing insight to have about yourself. Are you starting to understand your value and why you're here? Life has called you here as you are so that you and only you can live your purpose and change the world in the way that you are meant to. Once you realize this, you'll be all-knowing of your value. And you won't put much weight on what others think or how they value you. You will know your own value. Once this realization happens, there's no turning back. Like my life, your life will be changed for the remainder of your days. And this has nothing to do with money.

A friend of mine shared some advice with me that had changed my life. He turned my world upside down and changed it for the rest of my days. He had said, "Let them see who you are. Whoever that is let us all see you, the real you. You don't need to be in this self-made prison that you created for yourself." I get choked up even now as I think of that day, that moment when I became free to be me. What did that mean for me? It meant that if I disagreed with you, I spoke up. It meant that if I was upset, I would make it known. It meant that if I was afraid that wanted to do it, I did it anyway. It meant that if I didn't want to do it, I made it known that I didn't want to do it. It meant that I no longer backed away from confrontation. I faced it head-on. It meant that though I was generally a happy person, some days I was not necessarily happy, and I didn't feel the need to hide it and pretend that I was otherwise. It meant that I don't like everyone and not everyone has to like me. Most of all I was closer to myself, and being closer to yourself is empowering.

When I was in counseling for my marriage one of the most important things I learned about myself was to value and like myself. It all starts with how you feel about yourself and your idea of your value. It has nothing to do with what other people think about you, it's really about how you feel about yourself. And oddly this is something that may not come naturally to you, so you may have to do as I did which is to train yourself and teach yourself about your own value. And this takes time and practice. And as you start teaching yourself about your own value, you may not believe it at first. Oddly you won't believe what you tell yourself about yourself. As a matter fact, it doesn't really matter what you feel about yourself during those times. In the beginning, you have to go against yourself and teach yourself about your value. The reason being, in the beginning, you don't know your value; you've been shaped by your experiences and by your stories. A lot of times our stories teach us that in those experiences that we are not worthy. But the truth is we are more than worthy, we are just living our story, these amazing stories.

Show the world who you are and how proud and wonderful you are, because you are wonderful whether you realize it or not. If you are not yet proud of who you are, don't worry, there is something that you can do the change that. Only you can do it though. This will require some effort and faith on your part. What I'm going to ask you to do is so simple that you may fool yourself to think that this request is meaningless. Even though this request is simple, I must warn you that it usually will not appear to be effective at first. But this is not because of the request itself, it's usually because of you and how deep your dislike for yourself goes. But make no mistake about it this simple request will work for you, just like it worked for me and others that I know that have used it. Do you know why we are not proud of ourselves and think that we are wonderful? We don't like ourselves. That's right; many of us really don't like ourselves. You wouldn't know this by our actions because we are great pretenders. We pretend that we are confident when we are not. We pretend that we are happy when we are not. We pretend that we like ourselves and our lives when we don't. The problem with this level of pretending is that we may have temporary relief knowing that we are fooling others with our actions, however, that's temporary and we are living with ourselves 24 hours a day and 7 days per week. This means you for most of your waking moments you are silently suffering and miserable. Even as you pretend and temporarily fool others, you are still suffering at those moments. Not only is this an awful way to live your life, but choosing this way of life will deplete your self-worth over time. What's even more interesting is that you may not like yourself and you don't even know it. That's right it's possible that you are not aware that you don't like yourself. The reason why is because you have been suffering for so long that you are not only used to it, but also because our lives are so complicated with experiences and memories that we don't know how we got this way, and we mistakenly assume that this is just a normal way of life. But it's not normal.

I learned years ago when I was going to a marriage counselor with my wife that I didn't like myself. I was shocked when the counselor said to me that my problem is that I don't like myself. I never thought about it until that moment, but when he said it, my whole being and soul knew it was true, and I cried like a baby from this acknowledgment. The reason why I cried is that at that moment I had just found out why I was so miserable and suffering. I just didn't like myself. There were many reasons why I didn't like myself, but none of that mattered at that moment. All that mattered is that I finally acknowledged that I didn't like myself. And because of which I was able to start that long road to healing and moving to like myself. Which is what I'm going to share with you in a moment.

Our lives seem somewhat simple because we are here and exist effortlessly. You were born without your knowledge or acknowledgment. You are here and you barely know how or why except that you were conceived by your parents. You breathe, eat and sleep without even trying. Your eyes in an instant magically transfer images to your brain to decipher so that you can have sight. Your ears are able to transfer sound to your brain without your effort. All this can give us the false impression that our lives are simple and that all we have to do to survive is to merely go with the flow and just exist. Our life doesn't work this way. You can't just go with the flow. You have to have some awareness of your life and your environment and how your experiences are affecting you. This takes effort and can deplete your energy source at times. But this will also empower you, and give you some control over your life.   Really our lives and our existence are extremely complicated.   There is so much about ourselves and our worlds that we don't understand.   There is an endless amount of activity in our worlds, that we may or may not be aware of, that is actually affecting and shaping our existence.   Much of which, you are going to need to make a mental stand so as to guide and to direct your life.   I'll get to that stand in just a moment.

So in these difficult situations, I'm asking you to do something that maybe one of the hardest things you've ever had to do.   It's going to seem like what I'm asking you to do is to lie to yourself.   When you are feeling low self-worth or having a bad day, I want you in these situations to say these simple words.   "I like myself."   These are one of the most important words that you can say to yourself.   "I like myself."   It seems odd, especially for those like me who did not like themselves and had low self-worth for numerous reasons.   But those words saved my life.   And I believe it will save yours.   I've learned this from a counselor.   Think about these words "I like myself."   When you first start using the words you won't believe them. When you say the words "I like myself."   You'll actually feel that it's a waste of time.   But it's not.   Because eventually if you say it enough you'll start to believe it. The change is so gradual that you won't really realize that it is occurring.   But one day you'll look up and you'll notice a difference.   You'll come to realize that you are starting to like yourself.   You'll start to notice things that you like about yourself. For example your laugh. Maybe before you were embarrassed by your laugh because it was loud, but now you learned to like your laugh. And for those who comment about your laugh, you'll shrug it off and say to yourself it doesn't matter to me if someone else doesn't like it, I do. Or maybe you're not as interested in sports as is the case with myself. So when people gather around and talk about the big Sunday games and you don't have comments because you didn't watch, and the people tease you, you shrug it off and say to yourself I like myself, and I'm okay with myself and my lack of interest in sports.

This process takes time but it works. It doesn't happen overnight. It's not going to be that easy for you. It wasn't for me. It won't solve all your problems. But it solves a very important problem. This is you learning that you are valuable, that you are important. And you don't have to wait until you get a million dollars to become important. You don't have to wait until you have that sports car. You don't have to wait until you are perfect to have this value. You don't have to pretend and fool people that you are perfect or that you are somebody that you are not. You can have this value right now, today as you are. As imperfect as you are you can have this value now.

This is your homework. It's not a difficult assignment, but then it is. You'll tell yourself as I did there is no way this will help me. But it will. It will take time but it will help.

When you get your feelings hurt, and you start to feel down on yourself, stop at that moment and say to yourself. "I like myself, I like myself, I like myself." When you get up in the morning that first thing you say when you see yourself in that mirror. "I like myself." Just do it, for this is the foundation for all that you want. Why shouldn't you like yourself, you have already proven by your stories that you are an amazing person.

Liking yourself is a start and is so empowering. Liking yourself is not enough but this a great start. Imagine the impact that you will have on your family, friends or work if you like yourself. If you like yourself, guess what happens to your environment or world? Guess what happens to your perspective on how you see the world? Guess what you just did by this one act? You changed the world. You changed your world. You changed your perspective on how you feel about yourself which changes your world.

What did you really change? You still have the same job or not. You still have the same friends. Your parents are the same parents. You still make the same money. You still have the same stories or past, but now you are somehow different. You feel different about yourself. And if you feel different about yourself, you'll feel different about everything else. You see, it starts with you. A simple but difficult step to take. But you can take it. You know how I know when I don't really know you?

Because I feel that we all can take this step. We all can, which includes you. Remember, "I like myself, I like myself." Keep saying it until the day will come when you don't need to say it anymore. And that day will come.

YOU'RE NOT AN ACCIDENT

"You are not an accident. You are one of a kind. Your big dream is from God, and it's irreplaceable. And you were born to seize it and celebrate it every day of your life! -Bruce Wilkinson

You're not an accident, maybe you've heard this before. When I was growing up me and my brother were teasing my younger brother, and we explained to him that because he was the youngest that he was actually an accident. My parents who had overheard us laughed and explained that all of us were accidents and that none of us were planned. I was actually surprised to hear that. Has someone told you or made you feel like you are an accident? Maybe your circumstances have led you to believe that you are an accident. Some of you are adopted, others grew up in foster homes, and others live in poverty. Minorities sometimes who can carry a burden of society who feel like people don't value them can believe that they are an accident. None of this is true. None of us are accidents, though it may appear so as we struggle through our lives.

I've heard people say before that we are not an accident, but it's so hard to comprehend what we actually are and what our place is in this world. Our minds are almost not capable of that type of comprehension and understanding. I'm not even pretending that I have a real understanding of this because I don't. We've previously talked about your world and how your actions can have an impact and change your world. This world of yours could be your neighborhood, your work or your family. Our view of the world is limited by our experience. You are basically having a perception of your world as far as you can see, think and visualize. Even so, those thoughts are limited by your experience and perceptions and therefore your world is limited. What has helped us to expand our knowledge of the world is the media, such as television, newspapers, and the Internet. This has all helped us to expand our knowledge of the world so that we can understand a bit more of what is going on out there, but how far can we really see? Though we can see a lot with the media, it is still limited. Through the information from the various media types, we are still not really able to experience other people's worlds.

When I think of myself, my world is very limited. I currently live in a city in Colorado with a population of 106,114. With all who live in this city, they all have their own experience and perceptions of their world. I have very limited access to almost all of these people. Some are my neighbors, I see others in traffic, in the grocery stores, restaurants or wherever I go. Even so, I'm limited in my experience. Overall from my experience in this area since 2004, I find most of the people that I come across are polite and respectful of one another. I don't have the capability to visit all the residents in this city to find out their mindset of their world. But the ones that I have briefly come across I have come up with my limited interpretation of this area based on the experience that I have. I sometimes will get feedback from others that have traveled to other locations, states or countries to get their interpretation of their experience.

Man has created technology to help us expand our vision about the world, but though this technology has advanced over the years it is still limited as far as helping us to understand more about the places and people around us. Just in the area where I live, me and my wife like to go out to eat at our favorite restaurants. We sometimes talk about how we wish that we had the capability to travel to all the restaurants in Colorado to try the different types of foods. We like the experience of going to different places and trying the food. For us it's like a mini-vacation, it temporarily takes us away from our lives as we focus on each other and are enjoying wonderful foods and service. If we had our choice we would have this experience in every other restaurant in town.   This is not possible for us. We don't have the time or the financial resources to do so.

As you can imagine this is also how the world works as well. If you have limited access to your own neighborhood, think how limited our access is to the world. At least in your neighborhood, you are interacting with the people in your neighborhood, where there is traffic, grocery stores or in restaurants. Your neighbors though you may not have extensive conversations with them, you may wave to them as they pass you by. You at the very least have a feel for the people in your neighborhood. You are at least seeing them, experiencing their facial expressions and have an idea of how they may feel about you, and how you feel about them. You have this feeling of do I like it here am I comfortable do I feel safe?   And the reason being is they are at least in your view. But with the world, you won't have that same feeling of sensation. Many of us don't have the experiences to see the world its people and various foods and so forth. For most of us, we don't have the resources, the capability, and the time to visit these other worlds and to have these experiences. So our interpretation of the world is limited to technology, and that technology is the media, the Internet, television, the news that we've heard. But it does not allow us to actually experience what the citizens may be experiencing in these various types of environments in these various types of countries. The only way you're going to know about the world is through technology. But we don't really know, we can have an idea but it is not the same idea that you have in your neighborhood that you live in.

So when you think about the universe and what is the universe for us. The universe for us is unknown. It's so vast that our knowledge, technology, and experience are very limited on what the universe is to us on the earth. We have collected information over the years, but basically, we still have no idea what this universe is to us. We can only make educated guesses based on our limited research. We know that the Earth is spinning in the solar system and circling around the sun. So we are somehow functioning in this universe. And we on earth are functioning within the solar system with oxygen and the resources that we need to survive. We have food, water, and shelter. We are advancing in our technology and all this is coming from the earth or its atmospheres such as the sun or wind. We seem to have everything that we need to survive and to advance ourselves. So the question becomes is this all an accident? Could something so sophisticated, so exact so purposeful actually be an accident? The fact that you're on the earth that spins perfectly around the solar system in 365 days. That the sun shines in most areas for the amount of time that we need to sleep. Is this an accident? That the earth provides the oxygen that we are breathing, that our bodies, lungs, brains, and blood is structured to survive on this oxygen that the earth provides. Is that an accident?

Though I can't explain it, I don't think this was all an accident. Do you?

So if the universe, earth, oxygen, water and food sources of the earth are intentional, then I have to believe that we as individuals that reside on earth are intentional as well. Maybe even more so. And I say this because the earth has been around from 4.543 billion years according to science. The resources of the earth have been around for just as long. We as individuals reside on earth for a short period of time of usually no more than 100 years. I believe since we're born in such as short space of time compared to how long the earth has been here, that you are purposefully born here for a short period of time because you're here to accomplish something or to do something. And you only have that limited amount of time to do it. And I believe that you will exist for this short period of time because everything that you'll need for resources will be available to you at that time so that you can achieve your purpose. The people that you're supposed to run into for your needed experiences will be there. You'll also be there for the people that will need to meet and interact with you for their needed experience as well. The resources that you will need for whatever it is that you will do, will be there to create that experience that you will have, as it relates to your purpose. Because of which I believe that you are intentional. Every moment of your life is intentional, because you're interacting with others who are also intentional and you and the rest of us are moving towards whatever it is that we are trying to do for ourselves and mankind.

This is why you can't be an accident. Because our knowledge is limited we may convince ourselves that we are accidents. Now I don't have the knowledge or the technology to prove it to you otherwise. I know people will sometimes say prove to me that I'm not an accident and that my life has meaning. The truth is that you are asking for the impossible. Right now technology does not allow us to prove otherwise. Even so, could you be relying on technology too much here? Do you really need technology in this situation? Our limitations in technology do not allow for us to expand our vision of ourselves. But we still need to somehow expand our vision of ourselves and our purpose. This is more instinctive than technology. And that could mean that you're not an accident that you're not here to just move through your life with no value. When you have the understanding that there are billions of people just like you here on this earth sharing space, and there have been 107 billion people that existed before you, that your existence within all these numbers must be purposeful.

With all that being said how do we get confused and convince ourselves that we are merely an accident? It's the ritual of our daily lives that confuses us. Everything in our lives appears by chance. It starts when you get out of bed. You could stub your toe on the way to the bathroom. Was that planned? How about your drive to work? The traffic is never the same as the day before. Not only that, why is it that we rarely see the same people in traffic? The guy in the car next to me that was picking his nose, I'll probably never see him again. The lady who honked at me and made all the faces, I might not see her again either. This driving to work with all its unexpected situations gives the impression that everything is accidental.

How about the weather? It's never the same from day to day. One moment there is a gust of wind, the next moment there is rain. The sun peaks in and out of the clouds throughout the day. Overall, no consistency. The overall temperature may or may not be the same, but the actual experience of that weather, with the sun, fluctuating breezes will never be the same from day to day, week to week, year to year.

How about the people that you see? The majority of our lives is coming across and interacting with people that you've never seen or met before. Have you've noticed that when you are in your favorite grocery store that most of the people that you come across you've never seen before. I've shopped at the same grocery store for over 10 years, and I rarely come across the same people. When you meet people on the street it's all by chance and it feels by chance. Nothing is the same, and you cannot get your mind around that things are not the same, which gives you the impression that you are an accident. This is the same with my drive to work. I usually drive the same way and time every day on my commute to work. Even so, I rarely notice the same people.

How about our moods? Our moods throughout our days are numerous and changing. From moment to moment we can be happy, sad, stressed, depressed and all the other emotions that we can experience at any given moment. These various moods which will often create pain are our biggest convincers that we are an accident. So as we live our lives there appears to be no consistency in all that we are experiencing. You can even set a goal for yourself, and though you may eventually reach that goal, you will usually not reach the goal in the way that you had actually planned. Unforeseen obstacles will present itself, which may take longer than you had anticipated, and worse you may not even achieve that goal or decide to do something else.

A friend of mine's, who is an experienced snowboarder, went skiing a couple of years ago and had a horrible accident that broke her leg. It is these types of unexpected situations that lead us to believe that we are merely an accident. We get caught up in all that seems haphazard to us, and really this unpredictability is what makes our lives exciting. We really don't know what's going to happen from one moment to the next. You could spill coffee on your white shirt, may see the neighbor walking her dog, could get a promotion, and may even come across a book that changes your life.

This is how we fool ourselves into believing that our lives are accidental. It appears that all of our lives are haphazard and by accident. I'm not sure really why our lives are set up this way. I just think that we cannot yet comprehend or explain all that has happened in our lives because we only have a limited view of our worlds and ourselves. And because of which this limited view does not allow for us to comprehend how an action causes a reaction and it goes on seemly unpredictably through our worlds. When you decided to get up at a certain time this morning and you walked at a certain pace from location to location and drove at a certain speed from your home to your work, your many decisions up to that point had affected all that came across your path in that day, in those moments. That moment that you enter traffic will affect all those that are in traffic with you. The speed that you drive, weather slow our fast will affect the speed in which the others can drive. These are the types of decisions that you will unconsciously make throughout the day which will affect others as well as yourself. These decisions can be from the foods that you eat to the amount of sleep that you are getting from night to night. There is predictability along with cause and effect, but this is way too advanced for us to comprehend totally. And even if we could comprehend, this amount of data would overwhelm and burden our lives down. We are not meant to nor do we need to be burdened in such a way. This would take the joy out of our lives for we would not have time for anything else.

So the issue becomes that even though we are imperfect in this amazing environment in our amazing bodies, with our amazing experiences that we have created, that we will somehow assume that we are not good enough. That we are somehow an accident. I was watching an interview with Sharon Stone the actress and Oprah. And Sharon said something so important that I had to write it down. She was explaining how when she sometimes takes on a movie role that she feels a little insecure, and afraid to take on a part. But eventually, she will finally tell herself that she is enough. There is nothing to be afraid of because she is enough. And I'm saying this to you. You are enough. Whatever you're trying to do in your life, you are enough. You have exactly what you need to do exactly what you want. And the reason that I can say this about you is that life has picked you for this moment in time, with all your challenges that exist. Life picked you because you are enough. Life would not have placed you into this time period, onto this earth into your environment if it wasn't meant to be so, and if you weren't everything you needed to be to accomplish what life had intended for you to accomplish. I believe this is true regardless of how you feel about yourself, regardless of how others may feel about you or even if they believe in you or not. None of that matters. Life and its purpose for us are bigger than all of us can comprehend. Is bigger than what we can comprehend for ourselves, and is bigger than what others think that they can comprehend for us. Life knows what it's doing. Life knows who it needs in this moment of time to accomplish what they're supposed to accomplish. And life picked you. And that's all you need to know to understand that you are intentional in that is the reason that you are not an accident.

Though it is difficult, we must somehow step out of ourselves and ignore our emotions, feelings and our false perceptions of our worlds. We must have a vision that is beyond ourselves and our own experiences to have the understanding, that everything in our lives is intentional, especially us and our existence.

YOU ARE ALREADY GREAT

*"I am the greatest, I said that even before I knew I was."- **Muhammad Ali***

I don't know if anybody's ever told you this, but you are going to be great! Not only are you going to be great which I'll explain in later chapters but you are already great. Even if you do nothing, even if you sit on the couch all day and watch TV and do nothing, you are already great. Maybe you're thinking how can that be?

The reason why you are great is that you are born. I'm sure you've heard this before and I mentioned this in the prior chapter. Statistically with the billions of folks that were born before you, and the fact that you are here now among billions makes you great. It's the timing and place of your existence that makes you unique. But you may be thinking so what, I'm still struggling in my life. I get that, but the point still is you are already great. Realizing your greatness won't make your troubles go away. But it will give you an understanding of who you are so that you can face your troubles with a foundation of self. Go to the mirror and Look at yourself. What do you see? What do you really see? This person in the mirror can think and analyze problems in any situation. Weather this person in the mirror believes it or not they have that capability. It doesn't matter what you believe, that person in the mirror has a lot of capability. That person in the mirror can actually focus, analyze and process ideas in their brain. Keep looking at that person in the mirror. What else can they do? What can that person do that was given to them by life? That person can see, hear, eat and digest food. That person can communicate through language. That person in the mirror has emotions, like joy, happiness, sadness, pain and other numerous emotions. As you look at yourself, you have the capability to be aware that you exist at this moment in time. You are conscious of yourself and who you are. You are able to make choices for yourself, for example right now you are reading this book, because you're choosing to read this book. You are reading these words one word at a time or you are reading several words at once. Whatever your process, it's because you choose to do it this way, which again makes you great. After a while you will think and make the decision, no I don't want to read anymore and take a break. And you'll choose to do something else. That type of existence is greatness.

Are you great if you decide to sit on the couch for the rest of your life and watch TV? The answer is yes. You don't have to do anything or prove that you are great. Your existence and how you function in every way makes you great. You sitting on the couch for the rest of your days is a choice, and the fact that you can even see, hear and comprehend the programs on that television makes you great. All the miracle capabilities that life has given us that we continually overlook and take for granted. We take these capacities for granted because they are always with us, and we've done nothing to earn this initial greatness. It just is. This is even before we are pursuing our talents and goals that what we want to share with the world. You are already great before you even try to accomplish your dreams and goals.

Could you imagine tomorrow morning waking up to find yourself in the year 1600? Not only that but let's say that you are forced to live in that time period for 1 year. What a shock this would be for you. To go from all that you have today as far as service and products to make your life easier to what you will no longer have in the year 1600. No movies to watch, television or television shows to watch. No daily showers or even a toothbrush with toothpaste to care for your teeth. No internet, computer or even phones let alone cell phones with apps. No malls to meet and shop at, let alone transportation such as cars or motorcycles to get there. Not a grocery store on site let alone fast food restaurants. However, it would be in that time period that you would come to appreciate all that had been done to make your life so much easier, to merely have taken all this for granted because you had never gone without. Today you are enjoying what many nameless others have worked so hard and sacrificed so that others long after their passing could enjoy their products, service or sacrifices. That's how important you are. You are the reason and hope that all before you wanted to benefit from their service, products, and sacrifice. Could you imagine if I was to go back in time and grab an African slave from the 1600's and bring her into today's time period and show her how far the country has come with various cultures living together, working together, voting together, socializing together and eating together? Could you dare to even imagine how she would think and feel to see the respect that we as various cultures are displaying for one another? I can. It's not that we are perfect and don't have work to do toward improving our relationships and understanding toward one another. Because we do. But look how far we have come as a people, as a nation. What would that slave say and think if they saw how far we've come as a nation? Incredible, right? Her enormous sacrifice to survive and continue is the reason in part that myself as a black male can enjoy the life that I have today.

We need to think in these terms above to appreciate the value of our lives. Though we think that we are merely existing and passing through life, this is not possible. The reason is as mentioned above, that an unlimited amount of unidentified people that have come before you, have personally sacrificed in ways that neither you nor I can even understand, so that you and me could exist in the ease that we enjoy today, that was not possible for those of yesterday. Are you understanding your value and how it fits in with the world? Your existence currently and long after you are gone will benefit others. Unselfishly we have to understand like the slave and others before us, our names may not be known by others except by family and close friends, but our existence and what you do here will ripple for years and years to come. When someone tried to convince you through their own ignorance that you are not valuable, you as a soldier must stand strong in knowing whether quietly or not, that your presence has far more value than you or any of us can really know. But what we can know is that others will feel and know your presence without even knowing your name or that you even existed. That's how important you are. That's the value you add to this world. Most of us don't realize the value because we mistakenly believed that our value is our money, our titles or fame. None of that is your value. The most valued person to you and to me is the one that we don't even know had existed, but we are somehow reaping the benefits of the life that they had lived.

Now with regards to society, we will not appreciate you if you decide to sit on the couch for the rest your life watching television. You are more than that. And you are here for more than that. But even so, my point is that you are still great for your existence. But we need more from you than just sitting around enjoying all the products, services and sacrifices of those had come before you. We need a contribution from you in the way that you can contribute. Your life has meaning in ways that you may understand and in other ways that you won't understand. Either way, the meaning, and purpose is real.

So back to my question, has anybody ever told you how great you are? Well, you are great. I'm telling you man to man, man to woman that you are great. And you're not great because I say you are great. You're great because you are great. Instinctively you know this to be true. It's not that you need for me to say it because you don't. It's a reminder of what you already know. With all the amazing distractions in our lives from our own thoughts, to other people, propaganda, politics, and dangers, that we can totally overlook our value in this world. My words to you are just a reminder of what you already know. You can relax knowing that you are already great and that you matter in this world and that people before you sacrificed and loved you before you even existed. That's how much you matter in this world.

I actually didn't really understand my true value until just a few years ago. Of course, I learned this lesson through pain, betrayal, rejection, and failure. Yes, my lesson was learned through all of this during a season in my life. Looking back this was the only way that I would have learned the lessons that I needed to know so as to grow into the person that life expected of me as a soldier. That heartbreaking experience brought me to my knees in my own disillusionment of my situation and who I thought I was as a person. And worse I grossly underestimated myself in terms of my capability and my own value to my world.

What was my error at this disastrous moment? And I say my error because as a soldier I am responsible for myself and my own thought process and actions. Though others have an influence on me, it's only because I choose to allow this influence into my life. My error was that I gave over my power to another. I initially did this because I trusted this person. As time went on, I became suspicious as I witnessed instances that this person appeared to no longer be trustworthy on my behalf.

What could have possibly gone wrong in my experience or with my story? What I found during this process at that time was that I was not as certain about my capabilities and value when working with this person. I had the knowledge, the experience, and even the education, but I was uncertain of my situation and because of which I made the decision to hand over my power to another. And because of which, this person that I trusted, was drawn to this exposure like blood in the water of sharks and exploited my lack of confidence for their own personal benefits. Remember as a soldier I'm responsible for myself, and I allowed this to happen. I could have stopped this at any time, and I chose not to. It doesn't matter the stories that I tell myself of why I did nothing, the point is I still made the choice. Even so, remember this is a story, and I'm the lead character, and because of which it's up to me to figure out a way so that I can win. And I've done that. Even so, the worse part for me is that I allowed for this person, a person that I once trusted to chip away at my confidence and self-worth. I don't blame this person, I can't. Do you know why? It's for the same reason that you cannot blame others for what has happened to you. Because you are a soldier, and as a soldier you allowed this to happen as I allowed this to happen. I know this is harsh, but as soldiers, we are not victims. Yes, we do get hurt sometimes, and we can be captured and tortured by our enemies. Even so, we are powerful and are responsible for our own lives and what we allow to happen. It is only because of this perspective that as a soldier I was able to learn and grow from this experience. It's only because I took responsibility for my part that I had contributed to this act that had actually saved me. This situation was very tough to endure, and if I didn't take the responsibility for my own actions I would be a victim to this day, still a captive to this experience. As a matter of fact, I would not have been in a position to learn the lessons that life had intended for me to learn. Worse I wouldn't be writing this book right now, sharing with you what I've learned. Taking the responsibility saved my life, and it will save yours.

As I look back I have a knowing that this experience was necessary for my understanding of my value and capability. The lesson that I learned which I am sharing with you is this. Know, understand and appreciate your value. Because if you don't, there is someone out there that will expose your ignorance of yourself for their benefit. And when that happens, you are a captive as I was. Let me tell you, that is a miserable position to be. Though I'm no longer a captive, my life is not the same as it once was. I have the deep emotional scars from allowing myself to be put in that position. I had disillusioned myself with believing that I was helpless when I was actually never helpless. To believe that I was powerless when actually I had all the power. To believing that I had no choice, when actually it was my choice all along. When you know your value, others will not be able to influence you otherwise. Your value is not determined by others, by your accomplishments or even your education. Your value is your right that exists because you exist. It's as simple as that. The issue is do you acknowledge and accept your life given right to your value? Your answer should always be yes.

*"Honesty and transparency make you vulnerable. Be honest and transparent anyway." – **Mother Teresa***

To me, this topic is so interesting, that we are only fooling ourselves and we are not really fooling others. Instinctively people really know what your intentions are. It's almost like when your dog meets people for the first time, though they don't completely understand the language, somehow your dog through their interpretation of body language, emotions, and the facial expressions, are able to determine quickly if they like this stranger or not. They can also sense if the stranger is genuine and likes them or if they are not genuine and does not like them. We use to have a little dog named Coco. My daughter got the dog from a shelter when she was in junior high school. The dog was pretty friendly to most people. But the dog did not like my aunt. When my aunt came into the house, Coco would hide under the table and growl. Once she even charged my aunt and bit her. Luckily she was wearing jeans that day, so no injury. But what's interesting is though my aunt was a really nice person; she did not like dogs or any animals and she especially did not like Coco. As a result, Coco sensed this and did not like her either. We as humans also have this same capability. It's called instincts. It may not necessarily happen for us as quickly as it will for our dogs, but it does happen. We can often initially meet someone, and through this interaction, we will get an idea of what their intentions are with the relationship. After a while, we will know if they actually like us or don't like us if they are for us or really just against us. The difference is that we will sometimes have these feelings about a person and we won't trust it or act on it. Even so, people are not really fooling us about their intentions and we are not fooling others about our intentions. My wife has really good instincts when meeting people. And she will trust her instincts. Often she will warn me about people that I interact with, and later this warning will turn out to be true. Unfortunately I have not always listened to her, and as a result, I did get hurt sometimes.

We really think that we are fooling one another, but we are not. The fact that we move through our lives convincing ourselves that we are fooling others about our intentions is ironic because we are really only fooling ourselves. People know who we are or what we are doing. It's just us who don't realize that the people that we interact with already know who we are or what our intentions are. This is how we establish trust or destroy trust. If people seemed to trust you, then most likely your intentions are matching your actions. If people don't trust you, then most likely your intentions are not matching your actions. You'll see people pretending to have what they think is an honorable intention such as helping you in your career, but their actions will tell you that they don't actually support that intention but instead they actually have another more selfish intention such as discouraging you so that you are not the competition to them. And you know what? We know. We know that they are not being honest with us. They are just pretending. And do know what's worse? We pretend with them. We pretend like we don't know what their true intentions are. We hang out with them having these fake conversations about an intention that doesn't even exist. Our instincts are telling us all along that something is not right about this person. They don't like us; they don't want to hclp us. But for various reasons such as fear, denial, or possible exclusion, we ignore this instinct and pretend as if nothing is wrong. A horrible way to live. A mere prisoner.

I once led a successful project. The key to this success was my intention. My focus was the project and how the project could have an impact on the target audience. The goal was to make a difference to this targeted audience. I felt that we accomplished that. As a leader, I was intentional on how I respected, valued and relied on my project teammates. I shared my intentions for the project with the team which was to have an impact on our targeted audience. As result of my verbal intention and buy-in from the team, every decision and action was focused toward having an impact. Not only that, I made sure that credit of the project was spread among the group. I didn't take credit for anything. The reason being is because what the group didn't know was not only did I want to have an impact on the target audience, but I just as importantly wanted to have an impact on the team for their efforts. I did this by making sure that all of the team members were utilized, and that those efforts were publicly acknowledged and that the success of the project was given to the group, not me. I wanted the team to have pride in their accomplishments. Though I did not speak it I felt the group knew that I cared for them and wanted to have an impact on them.

Whether the project was successful or not is irrelevant. The project could have been a failure, but that wouldn't change my point about my intention at that time. People can have a deceiving intention and still have a seemly successful team or project. Usually not for long though. I was once part of another project as a teammate. There were about 10 or 12 members at that time. Immediately I found that the lead's message didn't seem to follow his actions. Though he often said that his intentions were about the project, the team and the company, it appeared through his actions that it was more about him and advancing his career. Nothing wrong with having the goal of advancing one's career. Many of us may have this goal. The point is it appeared to be that his intention all along was to take on this project so as to advance his career. Though he had previously said that his intention was the project, the team, and the company, he often ignored those opportunities and yet made sure that the spotlight and attention were always on him. There was a time when he thanked the group for their efforts, and in actuality, most of the group did not participate. He did most of the activities himself. He seemed to want to make sure he got the recognition and credit for the project. I found this approach deflating. But you know what; he did get recognized and promoted. This happens sometimes. The point is the lead may or may not be aware that the team could sense his true intentions by his actions. Absolutely nothing wrong with having ambition for one's career. I'm just saying that we are not really fooling anybody with our ambitions. People know what we want. Even If we don't know exactly what your intention is, we will know what it isn't. And your intention is not what you said and pretended that it was. And at that moment when we suspect through our instincts that your intention is not what you presented to be, we will distrust you. That group that I was a part of, I eventually left because of the distrust that I couldn't get past.

I once applied for a job that I wasn't initially interested until I found out how much the position paid. There was nothing about this job that interested me accept the money. And I needed the money. So I applied and it was a disaster. Not the job, because I didn't get the job. The interview itself was the disaster. One of the worst interviews that I had been through. It was more like an interrogation than an interview. Keep in mind I was focused on that salary and didn't really have an interest in the job. During the interview, I tried to pretend that I was interested in the job, but the two interviewers seemed to know different. Though I never through the interrogation/interview admitted that I was only applying for the money, they still knew. I didn't fool anybody why I was there.

Sometimes people will not have good intentions when they first meet you. Upon that first meeting, they may make up their minds that they don't like you. There could be many reasons why someone could meet you and decide that they don't like you. But we don't care about that. The point is our instincts will tell us upon that first meeting or upon a meeting with someone that for whatever reason they don't like us. When we sense that people don't like us, then we want to be aware that they may try to hurt us, or they may just want to compete with you, or they may do nothing. Regardless listen to your instincts, that whisper that may be warning you. Often I have gotten myself into trouble when I overlooked or did not listen to my instincts that were whispering to me. I guess I didn't trust it. But I knew it was true. I knew my instincts were correct. I was afraid to act on them or maybe that I was even wrong. But I usually found out later that my instincts were correct, and I paid dearly for choosing to ignore them.

People that are intending to hurt you they will not usually come as they are. They will instead come to you disguised as a pretender. This disguise will be in many forms, a potential friend, a caring co-worker, a nice stranger, a supportive boss, just to name a few. I was often conflicted by this approach. That person that is smiling and telling me that I can trust them often confused me, because at those moments my instincts would whisper to me not to trust that person. And I would look at this smiling person, with all their promises and say to myself, how could I distrust this person. There is no way that this person is going to try to hurt me. Well, guess what? They did hurt me. My instincts were once again right. And I once again ignored their warning. And I paid dearly once again. When will I learn, I would say to myself. When will I just learn? Though I love people, and my interaction with most people are pleasant, there are still a few interactions that will bring me pain and regret. And I never expect it really, not until my instincts tell me such.

There is the other side of this as well. It's those that are the pretenders and their intentions are to be someone that we know they know that they are not. I have news for you, pretenders don't usually fool people. Well, you can fool people for a little while, but not for the long while. Not for the distance that is required for long-term relationships or to lead a group or team for the long term. When a pretender is performing for out benefit our instincts will start to stir inside of us. We instinctively know that something is not right with this person. We may not be able to specifically narrow down exactly what it is. But we will know through our feelings that something is not right. This doesn't necessarily mean that a danger is in front of us. It could just mean that we are looking at a person who appears to be out of character with their true nature. This will make us not trust you, and not want to be associated with you unless absolutely necessary. I worked for someone once, that though I couldn't put my finger on it, I didn't trust the person. I felt that not only were they not honest with me, but they were actually pursuing to hurt me personally with my reputation within the company. I couldn't narrow down the specifics nor could I prove, but my instincts at certain times we would whisper to me about the deception of the person at certain moments in my life. And you know I found out later that my instincts were right about the person and all their deception. What I don't know is the details. You know, why did she do it? Why did she go to such trouble to hurt me and my career with this company? I don't think I'll ever get that answer. And it doesn't matter anyway. You know why? I had the opportunity through my instincts to protect myself, and I ignored those instincts and did nothing. I let it all happen. But I learned. Pain and disappointment can be our best teacher. Sometimes it's the only way that I'll learn. I now appreciate my instincts. I'm even at the point when I hear the whisper I'll act on it immediately. Often I won't even think about it. If I hear the whisper, I just go with it. Besides I've also learned that the reason that my prior boss chose to do what she did, had less to do with me, and was about herself and who she was. I don't have enough energy or the time to try to dissect why she acted the way she did. I'll save this energy and time for myself and my own problems.

When we come across a pretender just know we may not confront you, we may not say anything to you, but we know you are not who you say you are. Why do we not confront pretenders? A relationship with a pretender can be dishonest and superficial. My prior boss through her actions of betrayal destroyed all possible trust with me. And even so, I don't think she cared or valued this trust. No reason for me to confront, though I actually did once. The best choice for me was to leave this situation. Not by my choice. Our company made some changes, and as a result, I was put on another team. A life changer to be out of that situation. I thought I was being tough by staying in this hurtful situation. I wasn't tough, I was stupid. The longer I stayed the more I doubted myself, my abilities and contributions that I could make to this company. Like I said before, sometimes I'll only learn through my painful experiences.

Speaking of intention, I was at a seminar once. I sat at a table with 6 other guests. We all had our stick-on name tags on our shirts. There was a man that took upon himself to talk to the table. Nothing wrong with this, right? Except, he was using all of our names over and over as if he knew us. Even if I knew everyone at the table I would rarely use their names. It was odd. He came across as insincere and manipulative. A tactic that he probably read in some book about how to hold a conversation with people. Just use their names over and over until they are fooled into believing that we are all best friends. It didn't work for me. As friendly as I am, I just couldn't keep talking with this guy. Him using my name over and over just because he could see my name tag really annoyed me. Don't get me wrong, I don't mind people using my name. I just don't want to be manipulated while you are using my name. I felt disconnected from this person. I can't really tell you why he was using our names so often. I can only say that it wasn't sincere. And because of this, there was no trust. Can't build a relationship on manipulation.

The other way is to hold back or dumb yourself down to fit in. People know when you're pretending not to be ambitious. They know when you have hidden potential and you're not tapping into it for yourself. Sometimes they will know these things about you even though you don't know them about yourself. Or at least for whatever reason, you want to hide these things, but they will know anyway. They seem just to sense it. They also know when you are so ambitious and want it so badly that you have a desperation about you that you may be trying to hide. But there's no hiding. Because they know, they may choose to help you to your goal, or they may try to stop you. Be wary of the people that try to stop you. As mentioned before, they won't come to you as an enemy, but instead as a friend. Their approach will be that this is in your best interest, but it never is. You'll know when you hear them if it's in your best interest, but usually, it's not.

They can also get it wrong about us. People can make an assumption about us that is not true. In fact sometimes not even close to the truth. I had a situation where someone who I worked with and trusted was telling my co-workers rumors about my character that wasn't true. This person was a master manipulator and was always on. Because of her own fears, she would constantly plant seeds of lies through her daily interactions. She was dangerous to me and others because her relationships were influential and she never stopped. Her approach was flawless and believable. She could take a character trait of yours and spin to a negative trait to a sympathetic listener. After a while, many of us caught on and we avoided this person as best we could. Sometimes after a conversation with this person I would scratch my head and say to myself, that wasn't a genuine conversation. Her approach, smile and voice tone seemed genuine but all along she was just planting seeds about others or trying to undermine me in some way. Very dangerous to associate with a person like this. Dangerous to yourself worth and your career if your work with them. This person seems to have no idea that many of us are aware of the malicious intention and harm that she tries to put upon ourselves and others. Though she doesn't fool me and many others anymore, she is still fooling some of the people of power and influence within the company. Since she is so believable her audience is huge at first. This initial audience could grow and expand for months or even years. With cause and effect eventually, they will through their many interactions start to lose trust in this person. But if a person is a master manipulator it could take awhile before people find her out. They will leave trails of pain and destruction. I find over time that this list is getting smaller. I'm curious if she is even aware that she really is only fooling herself. My whole life I've only had to deal with one person that I considered a master manipulator. This person turned my world upside down. But don't worry, for my environment and personal development this person was necessary. If it wasn't for this person in part, I wouldn't be writing this book. Before I met this person I didn't have a real understanding of oppression and the evil things some people could do. Don't get me wrong I knew it existed, I just didn't have an understanding of the pain, hopelessness, and resentment that can exist among many of us. Now I not only understand these emotions, I feel them and I'm a part of them and that's important. Why is this important? Because if you the reader are feeling pain, hopelessness, and anger, then you and I can now relate to one another. It is through our pain, hopelessness and anger that is our common ground that we can relate to one another. It seems sad, but it's not.

I'll tell you another secret. Life can be difficult and there is no changing that. Even so, you can still enjoy your life immensely. The reason why people are often silently struggling and miserable is because of their perspective about their own lives. It's about how are you viewing your life and that struggle. The reason that I'm writing this book is to give you a different way to look at your life. To give you another point of view. A point of view that I live by and believe in. This change in your point of view is what's going to change your life immediately. This point of view is hard to come by. If your environment provides, you'll have a parent that will pass on this point of view to you. Maybe you'll come across a mentor that will share this point of view with you. Maybe you'll read a book with this point of view. Either way, the odds are not likely in our favor that this point of view will be discovered and shared. This whole book is about having various points of view to get through your life. Particularly important for minorities and women.

In the example above with the master manipulator, who seems by her actions to think it's necessary to destroy people's careers and hopes so that she can selfishly protect her throne of status. She seems to want to be the only one in power and when someone steps up; she will use all her power of manipulation and influence to discredit one valuable person after another. This is the point of view of her own fears and value in this world. You and I know different. Remember earlier the point of view that I shared with you as to why we are here. We are here to serve one another and to be served. This act of services is by those presently in our world today including you and the billions of those that existed before us and are still somehow servicing us today because they merely existed. You and I are here to serve one another and to enjoy and experience the service of others. We share this world together and there is enough room for all of us.

As you move toward your goals or dreams don't count on anyone. Don't expect help. Though you will get help along the way, just don't count on it. Know that you are going to have to do it yourself. There will come a time when someone who has the viewpoint of service will reach their hand out to help you. Make sure you take that hand and accept that help. Remember that person, be grateful for that person, and carry on the service. You'll often be in a position to help another, reach your hand out and help them just like the few that have helped you along the way. Remember we are here to provide service for one another and experience the service provided by others. A totally unselfish act. Even so, you still listen and trust your instincts. You won't be able to reach out to help everyone that comes your way. You won't have the resources and the time for that. But you'll know who you can help.

What is sad to me is those like the master manipulator above who are merely fooling themselves into believing that life does not exist past their positions in the workplace. That their only value that they hold onto is a lifeline is only connected to that position, that salary. And as result of this narrow viewpoint, all that life has to offer is ignored. The people in their world are not valued except for their benefit. And because of their position, they can influence and even convince you and others of their perception of your value. It's as if life has approached them with a test and said if you go against all talents and beauty that God has created, especially its people I'll give you this temporary status. What a crime to have committed. By now from the reading of this book you know how valuable you are. You don't have to earn it, it just is. And life itself is so powerful. So much we don't understand but nonetheless, it's powerful. Can you imagine the consequence that life has in store for a person who is so self-centered to believe that they can deliberately sabotage one valuable life after another for merely their own benefit? I do believe the consequence is powerful and final. I look at the master manipulator's life with sadness. We are not fooled, she is merely another pretender. Pretending to have valuable friendships, pretending to have a happy marriage and family life, pretending to enjoy her position and money, pretending to be faith-oriented and pretending to be ok with all the harm that she has done to others over the years.

Trust your instincts, they will tell you when someone is trying to fool you. Even if you ignore your instincts and are fooled, don't worry, this is just an opportunity for learning a lesson. When interacting with people pay attention and listen to yourself. Your body will tell you that something is not right. Your stomach will turn, you may feel anxious and uncomfortable. Stop yourself at that moment. Take notice of what just happened. You don't have to confront the person. Just pay attention and make a mental note for yourself and be cautious moving forward with all interactions with this person that had just caused your senses to come alert. Always trust what your body is telling you. Oprah has often said that there is often a slight whisper that is bringing attention to your situation. Pay attention to that.

My biggest regrets are when I didn't trust my instincts. Usually, we know when people are trying to hurt and mislead us. My issue has been, when I come across a situation or a person, and my instincts start to warn me that something is not right, and though this feeling is strong, I doubted this feeling. I made excuses for why I shouldn't act. It was just a feeling so maybe this was wrong. I didn't want to believe that this person that was in front of me with all their power, which was a part of a corporate culture that encouraged their managers to mentor their employees to grow and advance themselves throughout the company. I didn't want to believe that my instincts didn't trust this person that was a part of such a unique system that I bought into and believed in. There was too much at stake for me to believe this person in this system that I valued could not be trusted. I wanted so much from this person of power within this system that I believed in for myself and my family. I finally found a company that I believed in the culture and that I felt I was a part of something special. I didn't mind working hard for this company. I've worked for many companies, and though these companies were ok to work with, I didn't really buy into their corporate culture. Such an environment can sap your energy and happiness. That wasn't the case with this company that this manager had set off my instincts into warning mode. I didn't want to believe that a company such as this would employ a person that seemed to contradict the well-publicized company values of how employees are valued and treated which I believed in. With all that was at stake, I ignored my instincts. I pushed them down. And I paid dearly for that act. I paid for that choice. And the key it was a choice. But I learned. And you will learn. I would have rather not have learned in this way, but it was the only way that I would have learned.

I'm afraid it doesn't end there. Though I've learned a powerful lesson from the situation above, the worst part was not over for me. There can be a huge consequence when you don't trust and act on your instincts. The worst part is the strong sense of regret and the scarring on your sense of self afterward. The regret will linger long after you had initially ignored the warning of your instincts on a person or situation that had caused you pain or a failure. In my situation, I had betrayed myself by ignoring my instincts. Which led to pain, failure and a derailment in my career, in one of the few organizations that my values as a person actually matched the values of the company that I worked with? A horrible dilemma to find oneself. As result I had experienced scarring, which is when you are cut and when it heals, it is rough ragged and stronger. In that situation with me, it is emotional scarring. I call it emotional scarring, because I will never forget my experience and what had happened.

However don't feel sorry for me. Remember I'm a soldier, just like you, and through this encounter and experience, I learned a lot about myself. This experience catapulted my personal development and growth in a way that could not have been acquired in any other way. In later chapters, I will explain about my journey in detail about my personal development and growth. I call this self-promotion. Though my career was derailed at that time, I was able to manage and move toward self-promotion. Self-promotion is the participation in a vast list of training and education. This self-promotion has enhanced my personal development and self-confidence. A measurement and satisfaction that often only I or my family can realize. It's self-promotion because the progress and rewards are silent. The world will not recognize you or even acknowledge you. You quietly pursue one self-promotion after another in an attempt to better yourself, in an attempt to do what you love regardless of the recognition or not.

Though I would not want to relive that experience, I am so grateful to God and life for that experience. That experience has brought out the strength in me that I didn't know I had. Some days as I walk through life I feel as if I have this invisible armor that can deflect against those situations that intend to bring me harm. Because of which I find that some people that are trying to attack me will often give up because they are not seeing that their efforts are affecting me. Often afterward, I'm able to move into a relationship with this person of mutual respect. Not only that but more importantly I am able to face that leader that caused me so much pain and harm with forgiveness. And the reason that I can do this is that through those experiences I'm able to realize my power and strength, and as a soldier, I am not a victim. And neither are you. Though I'm silent in my experiences and growth, though I'm humble as I move through my life, I'm not fooling anyone about who I really am as a soldier and neither are you.

So it's about perspective. You changed your perspective you change your life. The situation is that I went through a difficult time and I made some mistakes of not confronting and trusting my instincts. But I learned. So you are only fooling yourself but you're not fooling others. People see your intentions and they know what you want. So don't hide it and don't hide from them. Also, make sure you are paying attention to other people's intentions especially as it relates to you. As Oprah once said, you'll hear the whisper when something is not right. Make sure you trust that whisper. It's your instincts trying to warn you. Make sure you act on this warning. That's what a soldier would do, and you are that soldier now.

WHEN THEY DON'T RECOGNIZE YOUR ACCOMPLISHMENTS

*"Talk to yourself about your successes; be sure you are recognizing your own accomplishments, no matter how small they may be." - **Rhett Power***

Often they will not recognize you for your accomplishments. Have you ever felt this way? I have. Sometimes it seems that they are so competitive and self-centered that when you have an accomplishment or success, they will go out of their way to discredit you or even minimize what you've done. Among minorities and women, this can occur more than I would like to admit. It's an interesting dilemma to be in and it's very hurtful. It's not only happened to me, but I've seen this happen to others as well. Oddly I've seen a sizeable population ban together to discredit my numerous accomplishments as menial. At that time I felt powerless and as if I was a victim of some sort. I wanted my contributions to be viewed as a value to the company. I felt my contributions should be able to stand on their own merit. That was not the case. I felt that I didn't need to defend my contributions, I was wrong. And that decision cost me. Yet another lesson that I needed to learn. It's not up to others to value and even to acknowledge my contributions or accomplishments. That's my job. Like a soldier on the battlefield, I must defend my contributions and accomplishments. But not defend to the nonbelievers. I must defend to myself, and move to understand my own value. I must fight for myself not to care about how others perceive my value. We must have an understanding of why we do what we do, which will help us to have a basis to defend our accomplishments to ourselves, when others don't seem to see us and what we do. Just because someone does not notice what I've done, doesn't mean that I should play along and devalue myself as well. Yet so often we do this. Instead of looking in the mirror for our own acknowledgment, we instead look to other faces for their approval in who they think we are. This approach is a mistake. A mistake that I've made many times in my life. Though I feel this path is the correct path to take for our lives, I'll have to warn you. This way of life is sometimes lonely and uncertain. When you choose to fight for yourself, often you'll be completely alone in this fight. There will be those that are not in alignment with your view of yourself. None of that matters. You make a choice. You either choose their perception of what they think or want you to be based on their limited idea of who they think you are, or you choose yourself based on your instincts and what you deep down know yourself to be. Though I understand this to be a difficult choice, it is really the only choice. Not even a choice really. You must choose yourself. If you don't, as lonely as this choice will sometimes be, you'll never reach your full potential to value yourself as the amazing person that you know that you are. No one can really appreciate you as you can yourself. If you make the mistake of choosing or valuing yourself through the lens of others you will have a lifetime of self-doubt. The reason for this is because others will not believe in us in the way that we can believe in ourselves.

It's difficult to know how people really see us. We can have numerous thoughts and emotions inside of us, that we are sometimes not sure if the outside world knows this about us or not. We all know that we are not perfect, but that doesn't seem to stop us from trying to measure ourselves against a perfect standard. Or worse we try to pretend or act as if we are perfect. The need to be perfect can hurt us. Especially if you are trying to get a promotion or an advancement in your company. I use to live under this false veil of perfection, and I merely fooled myself. I was once trying to get a promotion at a company that I had worked at. I thought to get this promotion my perfect history of experience, relationships within the company, knowledge through training, and education would ease me into the position. It didn't happen that way. As a matter of fact, it didn't happen at all. When I tried to apply for these positions they didn't recognize all that I had done, they instead focus on what I hadn't done. And they gave me these reasons of why I wasn't capable for the position yet. A perfect standard. This was unfortunately in sync with how I viewed myself. I felt and bought into the idea that I had to be perfect to get to the next level. So when I was told that I didn't meet this perfect standard, I went along with it. I would accomplish what they said that I needed to accomplish to get to the next level. When an opportunity came about again and I was ready to apply, they would give me a new list of perfect standards that I needed to accomplish before they would consider me for the position. This happened several times with this company.

As a soldier, I finally realized that it wasn't their list of perfection that stopped me, it was my own list of the perfection of myself that had actually stopped me. Remember earlier when I talked about intention and how people know your intentions. Well, I believe they knew my intentions as well. They knew at that time that I really wanted a promotion or advancement, and that I was willing to do almost anything to get it. If they said that I needed to take a class I did it. If they said that I needed to mentor more people, I did it, even though my schedule was full. If they said that I needed to lead another group I took it on even though my workload was heavy at that time.

But after all that do you know what that they did? Nothing. They just keep adding on to the list. I wasn't taken seriously, and it all felt like a delay tactic. Meanwhile, my peers around me were getting promoted. I watched one peer after another advance through the company as I seemly sat idle in my career. Hard to experience when I worked so hard for the promotions. So I did some soul-searching. What came to me in part was this. Man often will not recognize us for our accomplishments, but God and life will see all that we do. This was an important realization for me. This realization didn't help ease my pain, but it did give me the perspective and courage to march on. Especially after I would sometimes witness a hidden smirk on a manager or co-worker's face when I was questioned on my career.

From this experience, I found that I had a new outlook. Companies have a structure of who they want or think they need for the positions within a company. It's possible that you and I may not fit within this idea of what they have in mind for those positions. If so does this mean that all your hard work and effort is wasted? Of course not. There are really only so many positions offered by a company, and the competition can be fierce. Sometimes people can be judgmental of you because of your background, or even how you look. This can happen to anybody. Though this can affect you and your career, this is really more about them than it is about you. It's a limited way of thinking that judges us on the superficial. Over time as you implement yourself within an organization you will eventually break down some of those harmful views of yourself. But that can take time, and meanwhile, you will often take one blow after another to your self-esteem from rejection, misunderstandings, and judgments. My disillusionment with my situation often gave me the impression that I was in a war zone. It just seemed that I was trying to survive in a supposedly normal environment with nothing but unexplained chaos around me. Even so, I marched on.

The formal opportunities for the company such as the high paying and high profile positions such as the leadership roles were limited and offered only to the selected few. But the informal opportunities such as the low profile non paying positions such as project leadership roles, training and education seemed to be offered fairly to all. I fit into the second group. I received hardly any resistance as I pursued and took advantage of one informal opportunity after another. Because of which I received an endless amount of training, education, and experience in leadership with the same company mind you. Though I have not yet acquired a formal leadership position, I am so grateful for the numerous informal leadership roles and experiences that I did take advantage of. Because of which I had access to many of the leaders within the company. Many of which I developed a strong relationship with. So much so, that I actually privately scheduled moments to mentor with several of the leaders. I was careful not to take advantage of the relationship and ask for a favor in regards to my career. I merely asked for their advice and questioned them on their careers and their approach to obstacles. A priceless learning opportunity. Most people struggle to get one mentor their whole career. Through my informal projects, I had access to many. Sometimes if I caught them alone, I would ask a question or two about leadership and then move on. I would even question them at the wash sink in the bathroom if we had privacy. I was careful not to take too much of their time and not to put them on a spot with a favor. To do so would have destroyed the trust and the relationship. Even as I applied for formal positions and was passed over, I never complained or asked my many mentors for help. Besides, what they taught me was so much more important than a position. And what I mean is, I could have asked for their help, and then possibly spoil their trust and then I would no longer have access to them and their valuable resources. The trust that I'm talking about is this. Leaders that you mentor with would have to know that you don't want anything from them accept information and guidance. If they want to help you they'll reach out, but until then focus on finding out about them as it relates to what you want to do. I call this backdoor leadership. With this approach I have actually received valuable informal leadership experience.

I was once talking to a young man who was disheartened about his career situation. He explained to me that he worked so hard but he didn't feel that his efforts were recognized. He came in early, he took on extra duties, he often stayed late, and overall he felt that he did a good job. Even so, he was overlooked for promotions and raises. This actually went on for a couple different jobs. He just didn't understand the situation and wanted to give up. He had said why should he work so hard if his efforts go unnoticed? After he vented for awhile I went on to explain that his efforts were being noticed. I explained that sometimes employers will overlook you and your hard work. It can happen to any of us. Even so, life and God will notice and document everything that you do. There is nothing that you can do in this life that will go unnoticed. Yes, others can ignore you and not acknowledge your accomplishments and efforts. Some will even pretend that all that you've done has no value what so ever. And if you are not careful you will actually believe those lies about your value. It's a mine hole that you want to avoid as a soldier. We fool ourselves into believing just because we were not recognized and did not receive a promotion that somehow we did not benefit from our extra efforts. Life doesn't work that way. You will reap what you sew. However, often the rewards that life and God will give you is different than what people will give you. Sometimes you'll need to really pay attention to understand how life and God have rewarded you for your efforts. Often the rewards will not come in the form of money or even a promotion in the workplace. You will find however that you have been promoted. You have been promoted with more confidence, with more capability, with a mental toughness, with more of an appreciation of yourself and your value to the world. All of which has nothing to do with money.

Not that you don't still want that promotion in your career, because most likely you do and you should continue to go for it. I just want you to know that while you are pursuing your career promotion, life and God is promoting you in other ways. It's an interesting dilemma because when life and God promote you others won't necessarily know it. Even you, if you're not aware, will overlook your own promotion by life and God. Often this promotion that you see and feel will be for your eyes only. Others may not value this recognition and promotion the way you will. The reason being in part is when you finally realize that life and God have not only recognized but has also promoted you, this will create overwhelming emotions inside you. All along you have been struggling to actually discover, that your struggle and sacrifices have led to promotion after promotion. You just have to look for it.

In my own life, I have experienced this time and time again. Though my employers did not recognize or promote me in my career, life and God has promoted me beyond my dreams. Again these promotions had nothing to do with money. The promotions of life and God are so much more important than money or a position could give me. Not that I have given up on making more money or even a different position because I have not. I'm just saying that though others have not acknowledged my contributions, life and God have rewarded me anyway. And it's the same for you.

The mistake that we sometimes make is that just because others don't seem to recognize us, or that we don't get that promotion, we want to quit. I admit this can be a difficult choice, but that's not the time to quit. At those moments step back and think about and acknowledge how life and God are using these situations for your good. Are you becoming thicker skinned because what has happened? Are you becoming more fearless because you are sick and tired of being sick and tired? Are you becoming more comfortable with rejection? Are you relying on yourself more as you begin to understand your own power? How about the enhanced skills and capabilities that you have developed? If you think about it the list is endless. It's an odd thing that in my own situation where there was a person of authority that tried to undermine my confidence and derail my career, had merely created a scenario so as to allow for life and God to pass on to me even more confidence. I have never been this confident in my whole life. And the reason that I am is that of what I have been through. However, initially, when I was going through that situation I did not feel confident at all. I actually felt hopeless about my situation. But over time as I continued to march forward I discovered that I was becoming more confident. You have to understand that I've struggled with lack of confidence for my entire life. I believe that when you hit such a low in your life and you are somehow able to survive it, and not only do you survive it but you continue to march forward toward your goals and dreams, it's inevitable that your confidence will build. How could it not? I was promoted by life and God with more confidence. As a person with more confidence, I can and have changed my world. It is because of this new found confidence that I made the decision to write this book. And I'm not just going to write this book, I have other plans as well. And the reason why I am able to confidently and knowingly pursuing all that I'm pursuing is that I recognize and enjoy my promotions of life and God. And that's what this book is about. It's a tool for you to realize and tap into your promotions from life and God. Confidence is not your only promotion that life and God will give you. There is so much more promotion for you, but you have to experience and seek it.

I once knew a person that had worked for a company for nearly 20 years. During that time he had worked his way up to become a branch manager. He held that position for several years. With that position, he had the high income and the prestige. He and his family had a beautiful home and nice cars. Throughout the years though he was somewhat pleasant, I found him to be disconnected at times. For whatever reason, I could not really connect or relate to him. A few years back when the economy crashed, like many others he lost his job. With that loss were his income, prestige and his self-worth. He was unemployed for 2 years. During that time he had tried to find a similar position, but it didn't happen. Eventually, he made up his mind that he would take a different position that was not in management. As a result, he and his family sold their house and humbly moved into an apartment. I ran into him a few times after he had lost his job, and each time I was amazed by his progress and adaption to this challenging situation. He was learning about himself and was coming to the understanding that his value and self-worth had nothing to do with his income or the title of his job. Each time I ran into him I listened to his story and what he was doing, I found not only was I connecting and learning from him, but I had so much respect for him and his journey. What surprised me the most was how vulnerable that he was. He had a story that he was living and he told it without shame or regret. Not only did he not hide his struggle and his experiences but he seemed to have a strong sense of self. He had managed to promote himself through this difficult time. He often shared with me how grateful he was in his life and none of which had anything to do with money or a job title. He had become a soldier. From our last meeting, he had taken a different career path and had bought another home. I suspect that it won't be long before he climbs up the corporate ladder again. But whether he does or not he has been promoted and will continue to be promoted by life and God. And none of which will have anything to do with money. All you have to do is be open to it and accept it as it comes to you. And you to will experience the promotions that only life and God can give you.

SELF-PROMOTION

"Happiness is not in the mere possession of money; it lies in the joy of achievement, in the thrill of creative effort." – **Franklin D. Roosevelt**

I've learned over the years that there is so much in life that doesn't go our way. We can make all the plans and goals that we want, but life will often take us on another path. Not only that but we will often have interactions with others that will have their own agenda's and will not appreciate who we are and what we do. In these situations, we need to be careful not to get discouraged and to stay true to ourselves and what we are trying to do. Though there is much in life as we move toward our goals and dreams that we won't have control of, there is still an aspect of our life that we will have control over. It's an important aspect that we overlook and don't give ourselves credit. I call this *Self-Promotion*.

I actually learned this term by accident. It's an act that I do automatically. Something so important, that I usually do this daily. And I bet you do also. This is one of the most important findings of my life. This is one of those things that I was talking about in the previous chapter how life and God will promote you. What I discovered as I was pursuing one promotion after another and for whatever reason I was passed over by the company that I worked with. During this time I had gone back to school and had acquired an MBA. I had completed the company year-long program the leadership academy. I had successfully led some company projects. I had participated in Toastmasters and eventually became the president of the group. I was a member and eventually became the Chair of the group that brought attention and value to Diversity. I've gone to countless seminars on leadership and have read as many books on the subject. I've have mentored numerous employees and have mentored with countless managers and executives. Even so, all that I have accomplished for whatever reason I was passed over time and time again for a formal leadership position. I was confused and had to step back to look at my situation. As a soldier, I was wounded with doubt and discouragement. I looked at my life and all that I had accomplished and all that I could not accomplish. I felt stuck if not trapped by my situation. A seemingly hopeless situation until it came to me. Self-promotion is what came to me. In my darkness and despair, this idea of self-promotion presented itself to me. And I realized looking back that this idea of self-promotion could not have presented itself to me except in my darkness and despair. It is only at that moment in my life that I would have been able to discover and accept it. Any other time in my life, I would not have been looking for answers.

What I learned is this, when others are not willing to acknowledge you for your efforts and accomplishments and for whatever reason refuse to formally promote you, then at that time of realization you must commit and pursue the self-promotion. Self-promotion is when you continue to pursue personal development and accomplishments without the recognition and acknowledgment of others. You quietly pursue one accomplishment after another, making sure along the way that you are aware and acknowledging all that you do. It so important that you promote and acknowledge yourself, than waiting and hoping for others to see and acknowledge you. It's self-promotion because all that you do to improve and better yourself does just that. Even though others sometimes will not appreciate who we are and our contributions, we as soldiers must have an understanding of our own value and contributions to our own lives. Remember this is your life and your story, so it has to be so. Your front and center must continue to develop yourself and be disciplined enough to continue to go after accomplishments even though others aren't watching or don't seem to notice. I admit this can sometimes be a lonely path. But even so, it's a path that must be taken at times.

In general, most people may not even know about your accomplishments, except your immediate family. As you have one accomplishment after another you must take the time to not only to give yourself credit but to also congratulate yourself and celebrate your successes. Though these accomplishments may not necessarily lead to more money right away, it is still a worthy action for you to notice about yourself and you should keep track of these accomplishments. For example, if you decide to take a class on project management and you complete it. Oddly, maybe at the time, the company that you work for doesn't seem to appreciate this accomplishment that you had. It really doesn't matter. The fact that you took the time to sign up for that class, and that you took more time and effort to finish the class is a great accomplishment. It's an act that you need to remember and embrace for yourself. This is a new skill that you took the time to learn. This is self-promotion at its best. You are merely acknowledging and giving yourself credit for what you've done though others have not. Remember, it's still just as an important accomplishment to your life, even though others are not acknowledging it. What matters here is that you had the accomplishment and that you gave yourself credit. If you don't take the time to give yourself credit for what you've done, you will eventually become a captive to others and their short sided opinions of your value. Though most of us want the recognition for what we've done, in life there is a possibility that you and your accomplishments could be overlooked. This can happen to any of us. Even so, march on and continue to pursue those accomplishments while giving yourself credit and self-promotion.

I once knew a person who was disheartened because not only was he getting passed over for promotions but he felt that all his prior accomplishments with that company were not being considered. He expressed strongly that since the company did not acknowledge his efforts that he was wasting his time and that he would no longer pursue these activities. After listening to him for a while, I expressed to him about self-promotion. I explained that all that he had previously done, and what he thought was just for his company's benefit was also for his benefit as well. And though his efforts were overlooked he himself still benefited from those efforts. I went on to say that he wasn't punishing his company by not trying anymore; he was instead punishing himself and denying his own self-promotion. Though we want the formal promotions and acknowledgments from others, we must continue our self-development and progress regardless of what others think of us. And just importantly give yourself that credit for what you did. It's not just about them and what they or don't want. It's about you and what you want or don't want. All that you do whether others see you or not is always for your benefit. In those moments we must stop and take the time to appreciate and acknowledge what we do for ourselves. This is self-promotion. This supportive loving act that you do for yourself has more weight and is so much more important than what someone else could do for you. And yet many of us don't do this. And the reason that we aren't practicing self-promotion is that we are often taught to search externally for our sense of worth. Meaning that we only allow ourselves to feel worthy or valuable if others acknowledge us through their praises, with their money, and choose us for formal promotions. To prove our value to others and ourselves we'll buy the fancy clothes, the nice cars, the large houses and associate ourselves with affluent people. This type of lifestyle can leave you vulnerable. If anyone of these things above is taken away, your self-worth will go along with it. In these situations, you are going to want to look internally or to self for your own acceptance. You start with you. Once you have your own acceptance and acknowledgment of what you are doing and have done, only then can you expand out for external appreciation from others. You need that basis of self first and always. This is forming a habit of self-acceptance and self-promotion. This is a way for you to appreciate your life and what you have done regardless of what others do or don't do to endorse you. The endorsement of others is the frosting on your cake, but you and your endorsement of self is the cake. Without the foundation of you, there is nothing else. This person that I mentioned above has continued his path toward self-promotion, and as result, he has freed himself from the burden of trying to merely please others. As a result, he has not only continued to receive self-promotion but recently he also acquired a formal promotion with his company.

Even with myself, I have an understanding of my own self-promotion. With all that I've previously accomplish as far as my training, participation in leading several projects, the numerous books that I've read, the seminars that I've have gone to, my advanced education and the failures and disappointments that I have experienced has given me self-promotion in training in leadership. So the leadership is now within me. Since this is my self-promotion that I created for myself through my efforts, it can't be taken away. Because of which I conduct myself as a leader. I do this day in and day out even though I don't have a formal title of leadership with a company. I find this to be a very empowering and gratifying way to live. I found through my experiences that leadership is a way of life regardless of the title that you were able to obtain. I have watched some leaders with formal titles make this mistake. As they are dealing with their people and the challenges before them, they don't seem to be able to comprehend the depth of the responsibility for that leadership role. They operate on a superficial level as if that leadership position is just a job and nothing more. As a result, haphazard decisions are often made that affect the employees and the company. Leadership is not just a job; it's a way of life. I have observed that when one is a true leader they are not able to take off their leadership title just because they leave the office. That leadership role and responsibility seems to be with them in all that they do. I have found through my quest for continuous self-promotion, that even though I don't yet have a formal title of leadership, I am a leader through all my experience and learning, and as a result, I conduct myself as such in all that I do. This type of approach not only affects and enhances my life but more important to me this way of life has affected and enhanced my family's lives. Because of the example that my wife and I have set for our kids, they also understand and pursue their own self-promotions. They are living and enjoying their lives regardless of if another acknowledges them or not. To be able to witness my kids living their lives with such freedom is everything to me and my wife.

In my own life, I've never published anything before. I haven't even written a book of this caliber until now. But the reason that I'm able to write this book at this time in my life is that of my own self-promotion that I have accomplished throughout the years. Some of which have been taking classes on writing, reading books on writing, writing a journal for much of my life, having a job that requires me to write daily, going back to school which required more writing. This list goes on and on. All self-promotion. And I want the same for you. All you have to do is to learn, pursue and develop yourself. And you do this relentlessly while knowing and understanding that others may not be watching or even give you credit for what you've done. This is your self-promotion. This is your act of self-love and acceptance.

MAKE UP YOUR MIND ABOUT YOURSELF

*"You are not here to make others understand you. You are here to understand yourself." – **Kristen Butler***

Make up your mind about who you are and don't let someone else decide for you. If you are too trusting in this situation and allow others to decide who you are, most likely they will be wrong about you. It's important at this point to make up your mind about who you are or even to decide who you want to be. If you don't take the time to make the decision about yourself, others will step forward and make the decision for you. If you don't have a knowing of who you are, when that other person steps forward, especially if that person is of authority, you'll follow them. You'll follow their ideas and perceptions of who they think you are. And worse you'll open yourself up to possible manipulation by a predator who intends to use and position you for their selfish needs. It's up to you to decide who you are and what you want. Remember this is your story, and it's only for you to choose your own path and direction that you want to go. This is so important because as you live your life and move toward your goals and dreams you will often receive a lot of resistance. Surprisingly this resistance can come from almost anyone. It could come from your parents, a family member, coworkers, a boss, friends and a spouse. I've been fortunate enough to have had the overall support of my family, but you still may receive resistance from time to time. I once heard my father say that if you're not going after the dream or goals that initially scares you that you're probably not going after anything worthwhile. That being said, then it would make sense that your dream would scare or make others uncomfortable at the minimum. As you decide to go after your dreams you may find that the person that you are now is not yet the person that you will need to be or will be to even acquire that dream. This knowing about yourself and your dream can cause resistance on your part. So you'll not only need to decide to go after that dream but just importantly you'll need to commit to it as well because in the beginning stages of our efforts it won't take much resistance from others to get us off track. Someone could just slightly resist your efforts and if you're not holding firmly to your decision to the commitment you'll be captured and swayed into their interpretation of what you are and what they believe that you can do. One of the reasons that we would allow ourselves to be captured and to be swayed is because the resistance will come to us with logical explanations and with valid reasons of why we can't do what we were planning to do. This type of approach will sway the unknowing and the non-committed every time.

Trust your instincts here. Usually, it's not that people want to hurt you because most likely they are only trying to help you. Most people don't really know us though they will claim that they do. All of us have preconceived biases from our own experiences that will cause us to unknowingly pass judgment on one another. Interesting enough not only will our experience cause us to have biases with one another, but we will also have biases against ourselves. Both situations can be dangerous for your self-esteem and self-worth. This perceived bias is often why people can approach you with conviction as they attempt to tell you about who they think you are and what they believe that you can do. This bias in others and in ourselves is powerful because we believe it. It doesn't matter if the perceived bias is correct or not, it only matters if you believe that bias. We've all witnessed others standing firmly by their biases, and we are left scratching our heads wondering where that thought process even comes from.

Just as we have biases about others, you will also have biases about yourself. Depending on what we believe about ourselves these perceived biases can be dangerous to our self-worth and self-esteem. In this situation, if you are not aware of this bias you are merely a prisoner of oneself. This is how powerful you are. You may or may not believe the bias of another or even the world, but you will believe your own created bias about yourself. Often we will align our biases about ourselves with what others are showing and telling us of what their perceived bias is about us. If you buy into others perceived biases about yourself and make that bias your own, you are at that moment a prisoner of yourself. You are a prisoner because you believe that bias about you. It's that idea of believing that makes you a prisoner of yourself. If you refuse to believe a bias about yourself, then it is impossible for you to be captured by others or even yourself. This is why it's crucial for you to make up your mind about yourself. To have an understanding of your value, and like a soldier defend that value against biases that goes against who you know that you are. In your mind, you defend against your thoughts that want to continue to believe in the biases that are no longer true for you.

I worked at a company once that I was pursuing a leadership position. The approving manager at that time had a bias about myself which was that I was not of leadership material. Not only did this person express this bias to me, but they also expressed this bias to others about me. Because of the influence and position of this person, I adopted their bias view of my leadership incompetence as my own bias. Though extremely difficult, this self-bias of myself in regards to my leadership capability eventually changed. I accomplished this change in part by making up my mind about myself and what I wanted for myself. As I took the time to understand myself, I realized that there was a contradiction in the biases of that manager and the newfound discovery of myself. As result, I was eventually able to defend and shrug off not only others perceived biases of myself, but more importantly my biases against myself. At times it can seem as if the world is against you with their biases and prejudgments, but if you and often you alone are able to stand for yourself and defend against those biases and more importantly your self-biases you can march forward experiencing one glorious self-fulfillment after another.

I find that many people are not really firm with their bias stance with you. I call this false and misdirected confidence. Often they are not even aware that they are practicing bias acts against you. People can get their misguided perception about others from the media outlets, such as movies, television, the news stations and the transfer of misguided information from others. The media is very accessible and gives us a powerful interpretation of how we should view the world and the various people in it. Because of which we are all susceptible to some form of biases. We believe the images that we see about others, even if it's a made-up image in a Hollywood movie. These perceptions of the media will carry over into many aspects of our lives. As people interact with you they can carry with them their learned perceptions about you and your value based on what they have learned from the media and their interactions with others. It's a complicated and yet understandable process. This is so powerful and widespread, that this whole act of bias perceptions becomes a self-fulfilling prophecy to many of us. Meaning, if you are associated with the unfortunate group that the media has portrayed in an unsightly manner, often not only could you start to believe the portrayed images about your group that you are associated with, but even more damaging you will have ongoing unwanted experiences from others as it relates to the harmful media images that we've all seen. This continuous bias interaction can over time cause you to buy into the harmful perceptions about yourself as it relates to the group that you are associated with. As a result, you will limit yourself and your own capabilities based on the widespread limited expectation of the group that you are associated with through the media and the general public. This then becomes your self-fulfilling prophecy.

This often widespread misconception is the main reason why you must have an understanding of yourself and your own value. You must be able to analyze and separate yourself from your environment as it relates to the attempts to undervalue you and your self-worth. A very difficult act to do initially, but as a soldier, you can and will do it. What does this mean for you? It means that when coming against bias acts you defend it. Like a soldier you defend it. You defend your self-worth; you defend the misunderstanding, you defend your value and the contribution that you will make. By defending you not only are building your own self-worth and value, but you are also teaching others how to value you and your contributions. This is how you change your world and theirs.

So back to what I said earlier, I find that people are not really firm or even aware of their biases against you. David Maxfield calls this unconscious bias in his article "Tips to Battle Unconscious Bias." Usually, when you defend and bring attention to the situation, in most instances it will eventually stop. Even so, initially when you approach people they will become defensive and resists you. They may even become angry. People don't seem to be aware of their behaviors and how they are affecting others. There is a way to approach this which I will go into further in this chapter.

I do find that there is a select few that are intentional in their bias toward others and they have the tendency of pushing their unwanted actions and views on others. This can be treacherous to your peace of mind, happiness and self-worth. If possible avoid any dealings with this type of person, but if this is not possible then your approach would be to defend. You'll find that when people are deliberately pushing their biases on you that they are actually needing for you to agree with them through your silence so that they can continue to have confidence in their biased views and actions toward you and others. If you continually disagree or defend it, often they will doubt themselves and their views about you. They would not expect this from you and would have underestimated you and your perception of your own value. This would contradict their self-given entitlement of the perceived biases that they have about you. This may even affect their self-worth because their value in part is based on the falsehood they are entitled to be superior to you. If you act accordingly, then they may doubt who they are and their place in the world, for their premises for the bias are based on false information. Be cautious here. This person has a lot to lose, such as their self-worth and their sense of status and belonging to their world. When coming across you, who have defended who you are, will go against their learned perception of you in their world and create unbalance, fear and uncertainty in all that they thought they were. Because there is so much to lose they will desperately fight to maintain their learned entitled status quo. History shows that their tactics can range from exclusion, name-calling, humiliation, sabotage and even violence. When people are willing to push their biases on you, you'll find that they actually need for you to agree with them so as to have and maintain their confidence in this skewed opinion of you.

Depending on the situation this agreement on your part could be your silence, your tolerance of their behavior or you reacting in fear in their presence. I'll tell you a secret. In many cases when people choose to be biased with you, they will actually need your approval and agreement to make it so. This is how powerful you are. Defend, disagree and don't accept someone's skewed ideas of what they need and want you to be, so that they can live a lie to justify their own ignorance and mistreatment of you when that goes against all that you know that you are. This is your life and your story. It's amazing. So create it and live it with the freedom and power that you know that you have. You are entitled to this way of life because you were chosen for life to be here.

In David Maxfield's article "Tips to Battle Unconscious Bias" he talks about how to confront subtle unconscious biases. The first step he mentions is that we must **Speak Up**. Don't just bear and grin it. If something happens that leaves you wondering, say something about it. The next step is to **Make it Safe**. He goes on to say don't label or accuse others. Assume positive intent when confronting unless they prove otherwise. The final step is to **State My Path**. This is to describe your concern without accusations or judgments. This is done directly with no apologies, no self-repression, no accusations and no indictments. He goes on to explain that begin with the facts, and tentatively suggest what the facts mean to you, then invite dialogue so you all can learn from one another. You're not trying to attack the persons or persons that you are confronting. You are instead trying to bring attention to a behavior that is affecting you and your work. Though the situation can be serious and soul-draining, your approach is cautious and light. You are taking it upon yourself to create a dialogue that is safe for all. If you come across accusing and on the defensive, you put them on the defensive and they will not be inclined to see your way of thinking or how their actions may have affected you. In Maxfield's short video called "4 Skills to Confront Workplace Bias," he makes the point that when you decide to confront a situation to be careful not to take with you your lifetime of grievances. For that person in front of you is most likely not responsible or not even aware of that history and how it affects you. It is so challenging to confront unconscious bias without them feeling attacked by you. The key per Maxfield is to help others feel safe while confronting them.

Be aware of your emotions, anger and disappointment. Often when we confront, we dump these emotions on the person that is in front of us. After the dumping of these emotions, we disillusion ourselves to believing that because we expressed these feelings in such a way with all the power that we felt at that time that we somehow accomplished something. But all you did was vented, and this action rarely solves anything, except allow you to let off steam and give you the false impression that you may have solved a problem. This type of approach puts people on the defensive and breaks down possible opportunities for communication, understanding, and change. As a soldier, you must use yourself as a vessel for change. Not only in your life but for others as well.

What you want to remember here which can be difficult to comprehend with the weight and history of your pain and the emotions that may be stirring inside you from the encounter, is that you are not trying to win, be right or destroy others. To aggressively act in such a way can destroy yourself, others and any chance of gaining a bridge of understanding of the situation. As a soldier, this is your most important assignment and duty. You have to make a decision and commitment here. And it's a difficult one which will require strength, character, understanding, vision, forgiveness, and sacrifice of self. This is a difficult way to approach a situation because our emotions are screaming for us to react in accordance with how we think we may have been wronged at that time. This is an immature approach, and it doesn't work. The trap is in our own emotions and that we think that we are doing what feels good to us. This is not about feeling good and venting. This is about creating a bridge so that change can occur. The responsibility and burden are on you. You must create this bridge so that others will feel safe so that change can occur. The goal here is to create a bridge for a change. The challenge can be while you are establishing this bridge; you may encounter continuous resistances, hostility, rejection, and loneliness. These types of reactions can stir up emotions inside of you that push you to react accordingly. Overall you can't give in to those emotions because they will destroy what you are trying to build. Yes, you still defend, and defend, but not emotionally. It's these in the moment emotions that can get in our way for the long-term solutions. If you approach your life encounters in this way, you have empowered yourself in such a way that I can't even describe here. The self-power that you'll have, knowing that you can encounter all of this, even by yourself. This makes you unstoppable and fearless. Remember you are not trying to win an argument. This is not about winning. You don't need every situation that you approach to agree with you. Not everyone will agree with you. That's not the point. What you are doing is making it known that you don't agree with in act or treatment. You are no longer accepting or agreeing with the unconscious bias with your silence. Regardless of whether they agree or not, you have empowered yourself by speaking up. You are making a statement to your world that you don't agree with what had just happened. Again this is not about an argument, and this is not about winning. This is about you exercising your choice to defend or not. When you give yourself this power of choice, it is so freeing and powerful to your soul that it is hard to describe the euphoria that you can feel at those times. You are bravely putting yourself out there, regardless of if others agree or not. This is freedom and real power. And this has nothing to do with money or a title. As long as you understand this is not about winning and hurting others, you'll have the energy and skills to make this choice over and over for all the days of your amazing life.

I was once leading a meeting of about 12 members. We were discussing a plan for a project that dealt with a diversity event for the company that I worked for.   I unknowingly made an incorrect comment through my unconscious bias about a culture that we were targeting for the event.   A teammate spoke up at the meeting and corrected me about the comment that I had made. She defended her point of view so beautifully. She didn't hesitate and spoke up. We as a group discussed her point of view in that meeting and then we moved on. When she initially spoke up, it was uncomfortable, especially for me since I made the comment. However, she was direct in her approach, but she wasn't holding on for the win. She made it known that she didn't agree with my comment, and then left it up to me for my own interpretation.   Her approach had required for me and the group to evaluate our behavior in consideration of her thoughts on the matter. Because of which we learned, and our respect and openness for one another increased. It was such an empowering moment for all of us. Her speaking up made us better as a team.

Something to note is that we all have some form of biases or unconscious biases with one another and within ourselves as it relates to how we view ourselves. It has always been this way, and may always be this way to some degree. In all fairness, with the overwhelming vast information about the various cultures and people in our world, it is impossible and not realistic for us to have an understanding of how our behavior and possibly unconscious biases will affect everyone. This is why it is so important that you speak up in those opportunities when you come across a situation that is affecting you. This is an opportunity for you to teach and make known about a behavior that you don't agree with. Even after you have spoken not everyone will agree with you, even so, that does not matter. What matters here is that you are feeding your soul by speaking up and defending who you are. This will not only change your world but over time this act alone will change the world. As a soldier, your voice, your courage to speak up, your intent and your act of understanding, empathy, and forgiveness for those that have hurt you is your weapon of choice. Use it.

"Knowing yourself is the beginning of all wisdom."
-Aristotle

Remember who you are. It's so important that you take the time to remember who you are, especially during those challenging moments that we all will face from time to time. This act alone can maintain your level of confidence and guide you through those difficult times. The act of remembering who you are relates to the many amazing accomplishments that you have had in your life that you may have long since forgotten about. These moments can include an obstacle that you had overcome a few years ago that you had not thought about since. Or a moment when you were afraid and even so you faced that situation of fear and prevailed. Could even be the personal development and growth that you have achieved over your lifetime to this point. As you think back on your story, start collecting key moments in your life that you had did something worthwhile. This is not necessarily about making money or even a title, though it could be for you. This is much more personal than that. This could be something that you have accomplished that others may not even know about you. Either way, like a soldier, the point here is for you to fortify yourself with your numerous life experiences and memories of accomplishments. As you recall those moments of accomplishments, go back in time and feel the weight of the meaning that you had at that time and bring that feeling to the present. This is key when you are going through a difficult time or being undervalued. It is in these difficult times when we need to fall back and remember who we are. Often we can go through a difficult situation and we become that difficult situation, but in actuality, we are not that situation, we are merely experiencing it. What happens is that we get caught up in that moment, and feel the pressure of that difficult situation and then we embrace and become the situation. And because we are caught up in that situation with all our emotions, we forget who we are and all that we had accomplished up to that moment. At those moments it is crucial that you go back in time, and you revisit your story and who you are. And when you do this, you will be able to carry yourself through that difficult situation.

It's in those difficult moments that we want to take action to fortify ourselves against those experiences. This is when you silently acknowledge to yourself about your previous accomplishments and stories. This is a defense strategy to protect your confidence, self-worth and your dreams against a negative incident. It's in those difficult times that you will be the most vulnerable and have the most to lose as far as your self-esteem, self-worth and that continued pathway toward your dreams. It's in our moments of struggles and pain that we can lose our way. This can happen when you have a boss who is overly critical of your work, which can over time cause you to doubt yourself. Or when you have been with a company for several years, and through unforeseen circumstances, you lose your job, and now you are unemployed and searching for another job. Being unemployed can be a very hard hit to your self-worth. I once knew a person that had worked for a company for 14 years. During that time, she had advanced to various positions and promotions throughout the years. At one time she spearheaded a major accomplishment for the company. An accomplishment in fact, that others had tried to take on and failed. Even as she took on this project, she received numerous resistance and doubt from some of the employees that were involved. At one point she had to replace longstanding outside hired consultants because she soon found out that they were not capable technically to handle the project of this magnitude. At another time the project was tied up in the legal battle among the needed licensing agreements. She sidestepped them and hired another licensing company. There were members of the company that would not invest their time in the project, so she hired an outside consultant to help. The deadline for the project was one year. Many of the employees expressed often that this project would not get done. But do you know what happened? The project did get done. She actually missed the deadline by 1 day. The reason why was because she wanted to do one last test before she released the project. She wanted the release to go smooth, and it did. Afterwards, if you can imagine everyone then jumped on board and some even tried to take credit for the project that they were initially against and barely participated.

Her story doesn't end there. Less than a year later the company had a leadership change that affected the department that she led. They hired a manager over her and her team that she had led at that time. The manager was unusually nitpicky and critical. The manager did not seem to value or even attempt to comprehend the contributions that this employee had made currently and over the last 14 years. Within a few months of this change, this employee was released from the company. Afterwards, she was disheartened and expressed to me that she had failed and maybe she was not as capable as she thought. And at that moment I said to her what I'm saying to you. Remember who you are. Regardless of that disappointment of being let go from a company that you loved and worked so hard for, you must remember who you are. You're not just the person that lost a job and is hurting. You are all the victorious moments before you lost that job. Just because you lost your job does not take away the countless moments of successes that you had previously. Just because someone does not recognize or acknowledge your successes don't mean that you should do the same and pretend that it didn't happen. It did happen. It all happened. You just have to remember it. Not them, just you. She at that moment realized her value and contributions. And do know what she did? She brushed herself off and started that uncertain process of looking for another job. And of course, she found one. Really she would have found a job regardless of what I said to her or not. It's just that she can look for that job with the mindset of knowing who she is, without being destroyed by her circumstances.

Even with myself, I do not allow for my negative circumstances to determine who I am. I have an idea from my history and past accomplishments who I am as a person, as a leader. As mentioned before, I have previously pursued some formal leadership roles within the company that I previously worked, and for whatever reason, I was not able to obtain those positions. Even so, those experiences of rejection didn't change my perception of my history and all the accomplishments over my lifetime that I did have. My history and prior experience had told me that regardless of whether I have obtained a formal leadership position or not, I am an informal leader. As I looked back on my life, my history and experience have presented to me that I'm a strong student of leadership. I've met and have been mentored by many leaders. I've participated and have led projects. I went back to school in my 40's and earned an MBA in leadership. I've gone to countless seminars on leadership, and have read even more books on the subject. I've participated in a yearlong leadership academy program. I instinctively live and practice leadership with my family, my work, and my friends. As I take the time to look at my story, I've come logically to the realization that regardless of a title that I have, I am without a doubt a leader. This knowing is so powerful for me. Because I've taken the time to look at my own history, I don't even second guess what my stories have told me about who I am. So when a situation contradicts my stories and experiences of who I know that I am, I'm able to shrug it off with confidence and knowing. This is why I'm able to write this book. I have the confidence and knowing from my life experiences and the stories that have led me to share this information with you. Those previous rejections of my prior efforts can't change the fact that I not only live as a leader but I am a leader. So as I walked through my life I have this understanding of who I am and what my story is as it relates to leadership in all aspects of my life. Because I have this knowing about myself I am able to logically carry this confidence of leadership with me. And as I have discovered, regardless of if I obtain the formal position or not, I'm still the leader that my story and experience has told me that I am.

As a soldier, this taking the time to get to know who you are will require some discipline. When you are going through a difficult experience, it can be challenging at those moments to look back on your life and experiences in an attempt to get an understanding of who you are and some of the great accomplishments that you've done. Even so, this is a crucial step to fortify yourself against the grievances of life, so do it anyway. This one act will empower you, and give you the needed confidence to overcome and shrug off the obstacles that will come your way.

WE ALL HAVE TALENTS

"My imperfections and failures are as much a blessing from God as my successes and talents and I lay them both at his feet." – **Mahatma Gandhi**

We all have talents of some sort that life or God has passed on to us. What can be frustrating is that we may not necessarily know what our talents are at this moment or even for much of our lives, but even so our life talents are within us. I believe that we have life talents that are not only meant for us and our benefit, but our talents are meant for us to share with our worlds so that they can benefit and feel the joy of who we are and what we do. The talents that you and I have may or may not be the talents that can bring us fame and money. Our talents may be more subtle such as when you are able to help people to feel comfortable, or you are a great reader with good comprehension, or math and finance come easily to you, and maybe you like to exercise and you are the example of great health. Regardless of your gifts or talents, the point is that we all have these talents. And since the gift is inside of us, or with us, it will be up to us to search and find our talents so that we can not only bring ourselves joy, but we can also bring joy to our family, friends and the world, which could be on a small or massive scale. For some of us it will be obvious of what our talents are, but for the rest of us, it will be more difficult to discover our talents. Even if you are not aware of your talents, you are still most likely sharing your talents with the world and just don't know it yet.

It may or may not be so obvious of what your talents are. It's possible to get an inkling of your talents when you experience something that is of interest to you and is tugging at your heart. It could be something that you find yourself thinking about or wish that you could do. It could even be something that you have the desire to learn about, and that you are willing to structure your life around, and to possibly put yourself in a position so that you are working on these talents. I find that when you do have a gift inside of you, that when you see someone else with the same gift, you may get a feeling of excitement and say to yourself that I want to do that or I wish I was doing that.

There's also the other side which we may not necessarily know what our talents are. That's not necessarily a bad thing either. Even if you are not aware of what your talents are does not mean that you don't have a gift. This could actually be exciting for you. If you are not aware of your talents then let the search begin. This is when you start the process of experiencing and trying different things as you search for your talents. Though not likely, the fear could be that you may never discover what your talents are. That's alright because in the process of your search you could be experiencing and enjoying new unexplored aspects of your life. And those discovered findings can be very enjoyable when searching for self. I find that your talents are usually different from your purpose and dreams though they can be the same as your dreams. As mentioned in an earlier chapter, your purpose is everything that you do throughout your day and throughout your life. It could be as simple as brushing your teeth or eating your breakfast. Your dream is your future or anything that you are trying to accomplish in the near or distant future. Maybe it is that you are trying to get that promotion at your company. Or you've met a wonderful lady and because of which you have a dream or goal to marry this person. It's an action that is in the future. Your gift, however, is always with you. It's with you affecting yourself and others whether you realize you have the gift or not. If you know your talents, you can align your talents with your purpose and dreams. You can use your talents to help you to achieve the dream that you have.

My wife Christel is like this. She will often claim that she doesn't know what her talents are. She believes that she is not really passionate or interested in anything. Though unusual, what you are passionate about may have nothing to do with what your talents can be, though they can and most likely are one in the same. As an outsider looking in, I've noticed that she has several talents inside of her that she has continually shared with her world. Her talents seem almost supernatural when you witness her using them in her daily life. I have often witnessed my wife meet people, and within a few minutes and sometimes within seconds she has been able to instinctively evaluate that person's persona and intention. Over the years I have introduced her to co-workers, bosses, and friends that I have trusted, and sometimes after the brief introduction, she will nonchalantly warn me to be careful with that person. And every time, sooner or later I'll find out that she was correct. There were times that I chose to ignore her subtle warnings, and because of which, I often paid for it when I realized that I was betrayed by the person who she had warned me about. Though the betrayal was hurtful, the worst part was not the betrayal itself. The worst part was when my wife would say those dreaded words. I told you so.

Christel is an amazing mother to our 3 kids, which is another gift that she has. She is patient understanding and is able to balance between being their friend and mother throughout their lives. The kids respect her immensely. I've witnessed her come through for the kids when maybe others would not have done so, including myself. When my son was in grade school, there was an incident in his class where he was accused of putting gum in a little girl's hair. The Vice Principal called for a meeting to discuss the suspension of our son. On the phone, the Principal expressed that there were witnesses to this act. That night my wife questioned my son and he explained that he didn't know anything about the incident. She later said to me that our son is telling the truth. I had expressed doubt and explained that the Principal had said that there were witnesses. She explained to me confidently, he's telling the truth. The next day when we went to the school, she confronted the Principal and explained that our son doesn't know anything about the incident. To the Principals credit, she went to the classroom and questioned the kids about the situation. Through the questioning, we found out that the kids had lied about our son being involved. As a matter of fact, our son wasn't even in the room at the time of the incident. My wife turned to me with tears in her eyes and said, I told you so.

Christel is also a very strong person emotionally. She is actually one of the strongest persons that I know. I've seen her face and endure some unusually difficult situations and somehow she had managed to overcome every one of those situations. This didn't mean that at those times that she didn't feel pain, have fear or express her emotions because she did all the above. Even so, she would not stop and somehow managed to endure. As a result, we have affectionately named Christel the problem solver. If there is a problem in front of her she will usually figure it out. That's her gift. My son has the same gift as his mother. He is also a problem solver.

Your talents are there whether you realize it or not. Knowing your talents creates value in your life. This knowing will give you an edge as you move through your life. Your talents can be the foundation of your dreams. For example, I believe one of my talents is how I'm able to often connect with and help people with problems by sharing my unique point of view of their situations. I believe this gift is the foundation of my dreams to write, speak and teach. As I pursue my dreams, it's up to me to somehow incorporate my talents into my dreams so as to give an edge of uniqueness and value to myself and the world. We all have this capability. Even you. Especially you.

PEOPLE WILL NOT BELIEVE YOUR TALENTS

*"Just keep moving forward and don't give a shit about what anybody thinks. Do what you have to do for you."- **Johnny Depp***

When you are first starting out people will most likely not believe your talents. Don't be disappointed, for this is to be expected. People are not you, so they are not going to feel what you feel; they are not going to have your experiences and therefore they won't know what you know. As a matter of fact initially, when you are starting out, you most likely will not even believe your own talents. That's what happened to me. I just didn't really believe in my own talents. And because I didn't have that belief yet, I allowed others to convince me away from my talents. The key word here is that I allowed this to happen. It's important to understand they you and I are not victims.

We are soldiers, who are empowered, and we are responsible for our own lives. So as a soldier because I didn't yet believe in myself and my talents, I made the choice to allow someone to convince me away from my talents.

A surprising talent that I have is that I'm a leader. Not something that I necessarily aspired too in the early part of my life. I actually just fell into it. After I went back to school and acquired an MBA, I found that leadership interested me. I began to take on informal leadership responsibilities within the company that I worked. I mentored with numerous leaders and read many leadership books. The more I studied and participated the more competent that I became. Even so, I took some hard blows during that time of discovery. I received an unusual amount of resistance from peers and some leaders as I pursued formal leadership positions. If you can imagine this resistance caused confusion within myself and forced me to step back to reanalyze if this leadership goal is something that I really wanted? I had to not only think is this something that I really wanted, but do I really have the capability to pull this off? So I finally stepped away and stopped pursuing formal leadership positions while I tried to get my head together. I had actually convinced myself that I was done with pursuing formal leadership positions.

But I actually wasn't finished. I told myself that I was finished, and I even told others that I was finished, but my actions said otherwise. I continued to study leadership, whether in books or watching others. I even took on another informal leadership role. As I did all this I became more confident in my leadership abilities. So much so that I could defend against those that had resisted against me. What I found was that it had been up to me to understand and appreciate my talent because it turned out that others didn't believe in me at all. Not only did they not believe in me, but for a short time, I had allowed for them to convince me not to believe in my own talent. Now that I have an understanding and an appreciation for my leadership talents, I actually have a stronger riskier goal that I am pursuing. This involves writing this book and starting a business. This all came about because of the training, education, experience, and resistance that I have received over the recent years. I made the decision not to use my leadership talents to work for someone else, but instead use my talents with my own business, leading in ways so that I can help others.

We all have many talents, some are developed others are not. It's up to you of which of your talents that you want to develop or not. Usually, though you have a talent, you will still need to nurture and grow that talent so that you can impact your world or the world with your greatness. When I made the discovery a few years ago that I was a leader, I wasn't really confident or decisive about this talent. This talent for me was raw and exposed. When I introduced this talent to my world I took a beating. So much so that I had decided that this couldn't be my talent. But an odd thing happened. Over the years I continued to develop this talent. I joined a yearlong leadership academy program, I continued to lead various groups informally, I read more books in leadership, and I even went to leadership seminars.

My other talent is writing. When I share with people that I'm interested in writing there can be a danger that they may reject me and my talent. I've had it happen. We all have. You try to share with someone that we trust about our talent and they hurt us with their disinterest or even expressing that we are not talented at all. This type of reaction can discourage many of us from developing and sharing our talent with the world. If you are confident and believe in that talent, and know that it's yours, you will use that rejection and those harsh words as fuel to enhance that talent. Your talent can take time to develop and can take just as much time to introduce to your world. Since this talent is a part of you and therefore yours, life for you can be almost meaningless without developing and expressing this talent. I write, and this is what I'm interested in. This is what I believe my talent to be. Because of which, I don't necessarily need approval on this. If I share this talent with someone that I trust, and they express disapproval or disbelief, though I may be a little disappointed, I use their reaction as fuel to continue to develop my talent that is meant for me.

So what's your talent? Think about what is that you might want to do and don't think in terms of if you are good in this talent. It's not about how good you are, not yet anyway. That will come with time and practice. You're looking for what do you like, and what does your heart tell you. If you want true joy, you must pursue what makes you happy, and commit to it. What are you interested in and willing to develop over a long period of time if necessary so that you can make a difference in your life and your world? Denzel Washington, the well-known actor struggled for nearly 10 years before he made his first film in Hollywood. I'm sure people must have doubted his talent during that struggle, but he never quit. It's up to you to decide and to develop that talent.

As I look at my talents it's important that I don't compare myself with another. I must look at myself and my own progress. Just because I have discovered a talent does not mean that it has been developed yet. This can be exciting in life to discover a talent and now spend the time to develop that talent and to see the progress over time. And the day will come when you will share this talent with your world. As you are developing that talent is when you may receive the damaging criticism. People will express during this time that they don't believe in you or your talent. This is when you will be the most vulnerable and may not quite believe in yourself or your talent yet. You must remember at this time that you are in your development stage of your talent. Over your lifetime, if you continue to develop this talent, you will only get better. So this is not the time to quit. Instead feel the joy of that talent that you have discovered about yourself, and invest the time in yourself and that talent. It's the mere joy of discovering this talent about yourself that will pull you through all your skeptics. So when some go against your talents, like a soldier defend it. Defend it with yourself first, and then defend it against your world. Though a sometimes lonely and a hurtful path, this is how you empower yourself so that you can continue to search for and to develop those talents. Though I have not received the formal promotions and often acknowledgments of my accomplishments, I have still empowered myself by developing my talents. None of which have anything to do with money or positions. I want this for you as well. I also want you to have everything that you want in your life, including the promotions the money, but it doesn't always come timely. Even so, your talents will always present themselves to you. This joy of experiencing and sharing your talents with your world will give you immediate gratification and empowerment. Though others will sometimes not believe in your talents, you make sure that you do, and live your life as such.

THE FOUNDATION OF YOUR WHOLE LIFE

*"All success begins with self-discipline. It starts with you."- **Dwayne 'The Rock' Johnson***

Liking yourself is the foundation of everything that you are and do. Liking yourself doesn't seem to come naturally, it is actually learned. If you don't like yourself it's most likely because you've learned not to. The good news is this thought process can be unlearned. This is a subject that we touched on in an earlier chapter in the book. This is so important for your and my development that we will touch on it again but from a different angle. From the day you were born unknowingly your environment, your world is teaching you about yourself, including how you should feel about yourself. If you are fortunate enough in your environment which includes your parents, family and the media that have provided you with continuous reinforcement that you have value in this world, then you will most likely like yourself. But for many of us, that's not the case. Though some of us don't initially have the support of our environment in regards to liking ourselves, this lack of support can all be undone if you are aware. It's really not that your environment is teaching and supporting you not to like yourself that is doing you the most damage. It's that you are not aware of your own value and you are unconsciously buying into the constant stimulus of your world that you have no value. Let me tell you from my own experience that this stimulus is all a lie. It's not real and it's not your truth. The problem is that many of us are not aware of our own value and we subconsciously escalate the value of others based on how they treat us. And since the numbers are so large in this shared belief for either position; we are all falling into line with these shared beliefs about ourselves and about others, because that's what we see everyone else doing. We see the masses around us walking in their space of devaluing and not liking themselves. And since you look like them on some level, or share a history or an experience, then you too from a learned observation will also walk that line of low self-worth and possibly a victim. Again remember this can all be undone. And if you read the earlier chapter you know how. It's a simple step, but it's a difficult step, and it requires your faith and courage. The reason why it's difficult is that you will need to unlearn the negative stimulus or the lie about yourself, and that is difficult but very possible. This is what I had to do. There was a time not long ago that I didn't like myself. There are many reasons why I latched on to as to why I shouldn't like myself. We all can find reasons. The difference for some of us is that we like ourselves and ignore those reasons, and instead choose to focus on the reasons why they like themselves. This change in your thought process can make all the difference in how you feel about yourself. And how you feel about yourself is the foundation of all that you will do.

That being said, those of us that fall into the trap of not liking ourselves are not even aware that we have the choice to decide to like or not like ourselves. The process or idea of liking ourselves is shaped by our past experiences and how we view the experiences as relates to us. We are also simultaneously analyzing our present environment and how we are struggling to fit into this environment. Based on our experiences and our interpretation of the present moment, we will tell ourselves stories as relates to ourselves. These stories could enhance our self-image or destroy our self-image. Which is what happened to me. I chose to interpret some of my difficult past experiences as reasons not to like myself. And I carried these stories of my low self-worth into my adulthood. A potential tragedy for one's life. An unnecessary prison that we don't have to step into, yet many of us do. To me, it's an example of the elephant that has been trained not to understand their own power. So the elephant is tied to a post with a measly rope. A rope that could be easily broken if the elephant understood its own strength. Our minds often work this way. We are so powerful as humans, but because of our negative environment and our past experiences, we allow those experiences to train and convince us that we are powerless or even less than. The elephant and the rope scenario. None of this is true. But because this is our lives, our stories, our emotions, we believe it's true. We believe that we are powerless, we believe that we are less than. We believe that we can't make a difference. And then we believe that we don't like ourselves. With all that we experience, and tell ourselves, how can we like ourselves? Nobody else seems to.

That's the stories we tell ourselves, and that's how strong our feelings are about our self-worth. I use to be a sales professional. Over the years I sold many products from, cars, life insurance, office products, and appliances. An important lesson that I learned about selling is this, if the salesperson tells the customer about what the product or service can do for them, this can be viewed by the customer as not necessarily trustworthy. The reason, the customer doesn't really know this salesperson, they don't know if they can trust them. Yet, if the customer says what the product does for themselves, then this is viewed as the truth in the customer's mind. It's their truth because they said it. And if they say it must be true, at least their truth anyway. So they buy a product based on their truth.

This is how we think in terms of how we view ourselves as relates to our prior experiences and our present moments. How we feel about ourselves begins and stops with us. If we are telling ourselves stories that support low self-worth, because it's us we believe it. Like the customer, we believe what we tell ourselves. Our negative experiences can create a negative emotion such as pain, or rejection which will unconsciously cause us to have a negative view or response to ourselves. Over time you may choose to unknowingly to allow those experiences to shape your self-worth. I say unknowingly because like the elephant you don't yet understand your power over your thoughts. Because you don't know is not your fault. Life is extremely complicated, and there are an unlimited amount of stimulus and messages that we all receive in our worlds. It's impossible to know how to interpret these messages as relates to our own lives, and then what message do we accept or not accept about ourselves. And when you add our own emotions into the mix, such as pain, anger, and fear which are strong and can cause us to be reactive. So much so that we fool ourselves into believing that because we have taken an action to eliminate these strong emotions, that somehow, this was the correct action to take in the situation that we found ourselves. Yet our emotions as strong as they are to us can steer us wrong if we allow them to guide us. But many of us don't know this about ourselves, and if we don't have the knowledge about the potential trap of our emotions and our thoughts, then it's understandable that we take the view of low self-worth for ourselves. Some of us are privileged because we have been raised in nurturing environments that support and teach us to like and value ourselves. So for them, this idea of not liking themselves is not even an option. As a matter of fact, a select few may even go as far as to overvalue their worth and devalue your worth. And this can be dangerous to your sense of self, peace of mind and happiness if you don't have the mindset and the habit to value yourself.

I also find that so many of us are fooling ourselves because we think our money or job titles somehow create our self-worth and value and it actually doesn't. This may be hard for you to believe, but it's true, your money or your job positions does not create your self-worth. I sometimes see people with comfortable salaries or status titles go out of their way to make it known to the rest of us about their status in society. In some cases, it is as if they do not feel secure in your presence until they immediately tell you about their position and hint about their salary. Often they don't even want to hear what you have to say, they just want you to know who they are, and that they are important. They may ask about your title to see if you are worthy of talking with or to even position themselves to talk down to you. It can be hard to witness sometimes. This is not to say that all of us who have titles and comfortable salaries do this because we don't. This is not an attempt to downplay success because it's not. I want success for myself, and I want success for you. This is more to point out a selected few that seem to have some success, but they still show us examples of low self-worth. When you meet them, you know immediately that this person is lacking self-worth and is focusing on something that will not bring them happiness or peace of mind. There is desperation in their actions as they reach out to you so as to prove to you that they are valuable and worthy to exist. The sad part is that this perceived value is all based on a salary or a job title. This person will often talk about, their cars, clothes or just money in general. If you don't make their money, wear their clothes or have the car that they value, they will turn their nose up at you. They say or give you the impression that you are not good enough to be in their presence. Some of these interactions can be unusually obnoxious. I know someone who was at a friendly get together with some associates at the local tavern. There was a person there who was the boyfriend of one of the friends. He appeared somewhat distant from the group. When he was finally approached by a patron in an attempt to talk about sports, the person was abruptly dismissive when he responded with "I'm a businessman, I don't talk sports," and walked off. He had alienated himself from the group in an attempt to somehow prove his value. He really only proved that he was a pretender with low-self worth.

Liking yourself is the foundation of everything you do and will do. But how do we get to the point that we don't value ourselves? You can actually look back on your story and you may discover some key moments in your life that may have affected you and convinced you through your pain and rejection that you may not be worthy. Could be that your parents didn't value themselves because of the experiences that they had growing up, and as result of this, they unknowingly taught this belief system to you. Maybe a family member called you ugly and told you that you weren't anything and never was going to be nothing. Possibly you were bullied; this act sent you a message of your value. Maybe your dad left the family when you were young and this affected your worth. Possibly you lost a good job or you are recently divorced. Could be as in my case, as a black male I would sometimes receive negative and bewildering responses from society on all levels as I tried to interact with my daily life. These hurtful interactions would sometimes create confusion for myself as I tried to interpret what these experiences meant and why. As a young person, the only conclusion that I could come up with was that I was not of value to society therefore not to myself. And this was my process of creating and living my low self-worth for years to come. That was me over 20 years ago. A horrible way to exist.

Even when I desperately wanted the money and the position so that I could feel worthy of myself and to others. I deceived myself into believing that the money was the key to my salvation. It wasn't. Yes, the money would change my life so that I could buy things, but it wouldn't change who I was. Yes, I would have a bank account, a car, a home, but I would still be that same person with low self-worth who didn't like themselves. This is why it's not just about the money. You are more than your money, I'm more than my money. We all want money, and we need the money, but our lives and who we are cannot be only about the money. If your life is this way, then you are an empty shell.

As mentioned in prior chapters, as a soldier I'm responsible for myself, therefore, I created this existence for myself. The money never saved me. What saved me was my, thought process and how I viewed myself and my world. It can be difficult to get to this understanding about yourself, but once you get there, it will require your daily discipline to maintain this level of confidence. Your goals can still be the same for your career, the money, your family or whatever you want to do. You just need to change your mindset so that you like yourself along the way. Life is so much more joyful when you like yourself. Your problems won't go away, your challenges will still be the same, but the difference is that you'll like yourself along the way. And since we live with ourselves 24 hours a day, and 7 days a week, this is important.

The first step in liking yourself is just saying it. "I like myself." We talked about this in an earlier chapter. Tell yourself that you like yourself. Say it every day. Say it all day if you must, but say it. Say it when you first get up and look at yourself in the mirror. Say it when someone hurts you or rejects you. Say it when you are facing a problem. Say it at that moment when you don't feel good about yourself. "I like myself, I like myself." You keep saying it until the day comes when you don't have to say it anymore because you should like yourself. Initially, if you don't like yourself, this act will feel dishonest and forced. Ignore all that. You are teaching yourself to like yourself. This is where the daily discipline will come into play. You won't feel like doing this because you don't like yourself and you don't believe it will work. But it will. When I first started this a few years ago, I didn't believe it would work either. But it did. I also found that saying I like myself during my challenging moments helped me to get through those tough moments with a little more peace. Eventually, the time did come where liking myself was automatic, and I no longer needed to say to myself that I like myself. This sounds simple, but this is the start of your thinking so that you can view yourself as you should, a valuable person. It's our thought process that hurts us and how we interpret our world. Just say it. "I like myself."

GUESS WHAT, YOU'RE NOT UGLY

"True forgiveness is when you can say, "Thank you for that experience."— **Oprah Winfrey**

You're not ugly and there's nothing ugly about you. It's unfortunate that so many of us actually think that we are ugly in this world. We hold ourselves to the standard of cinema, television and glamour magazines. Because of these advertisements we train ourselves to buy into this representation of beauty. An idea of a beauty that may not represent your beauty, because your features are unique to the represented media. That uniqueness that you may have is a beauty in itself. When you have that foundation of liking yourself that we talked about in the earlier chapters, you'll learn to understand and to appreciate your own beauty. Even if the world's interpretation of beauty is different from what you are seeing in the mirror. And when you learn to appreciate your own beauty, you will talk, and walk as so, and your world will celebrate your idea of beauty along side of you. The key is it is your responsibility to accept and acknowledge your own beauty first. Like a soldier, you must fight for your idea of beauty. There are ignorance, self-hatred, and misunderstandings in our worlds; you must protect yourself against all of that.

When I was 12 years old, someone said something to me that affected my core of who I am and changed my life. Even to this day, I believe I'm affected somehow. Do you know what was said to me? Someone alienated me by calling me ugly. I was called ugly. For some reason, that word, that name really hit me hard. A group of kids said that I could not play with them because I was ugly. That was probably the first time in my life that my feelings were hurt in such a way. For the first time in my young life, I knew that I didn't belong or fit in with others. I never felt that way before, never had a problem playing with others or fitting in until that day. Never really cared if I fit in or not until that day. I remember laughing off the comment, but I wasn't really laughing, and the situation wasn't funny to me at all. So I left and I sat alone, and I stayed that way for years to come. I had friends and I played sports, but that feeling of not belonging and being uncomfortable with myself stayed with me for a long time.

Though I was only 12, I allowed my interpretation of this experience to convince me that I was not worthwhile and not to like myself. I made the decision to accept someone's opinion of me, which was that I was ugly. They told me that I was ugly and I believed them and worse I accepted it as my truth. And this belief and acceptance on my part deteriorated my self-worth. I did this to myself. Yes, you read this right, I did this to myself. This was my decision to view the experience in this way. Remember we are soldiers, and as a soldier, we must take responsibility for ourselves. Often in the short run I cannot control what others do or even say to me or about me, but I can control how I respond and interpret this information. The pain would still be there because I was rejected and therefore hurt, but it should stop there. I should at that moment take control of my thoughts and process of this situation with all its pain of rejection, and turn this moment into something that protects and benefits me. Through my thoughts, I have that power and capability, and so do you. We all do. The problem is that we are not aware that we have this power and control over our thoughts in these situations. It's our emotions of pain, rejection, humiliation, fear or anger that take over at these crucial moments in our lives. Our brains are protecting us and encouraging us to flee. It knows we've been hurt and it wants us to run. So we run. We follow our emotions and we run when we are in that situation of pain, rejection fear and so on. Because we are running, our emotions can be overwhelming to us at those moments. We won't take the time to take control of the situation, and at that moment to create through our power of our own perspective of our situations, so that we can protect ourselves from being influenced by others in ways that we don't agree with.

Because someone called me ugly, does that mean that it's true or even that I need to agree with them? No. I don't need to agree with them and I don't agree with them. It's not that I even have to respond to the offender as a situation occurs. But it's critical that we in those moments get control of our thoughts. You'll know when it's time to get control because your body will tell you. When you feel pain, rejection, humiliation, and fear, that's your indication to stop and get control of your thoughts. This will take discipline because you'll want to flee with your emotions. But this fleeing is our mistake. This fleeing was my mistake at 12 when I felt the emotions of being humiliated and alone. Though I was only 12, I am still responsible for my thoughts and how I interpret and process my feelings and experiences. It can be unfair because many of us don't come from environments that encourage and teach us how to do this when we are young. So we become adults who are struggling with our emotions, pain and possible decisions. As adults, we carry these skewed ideas and perceptions about our own situations and state of mind that is actually false.

What's interesting is when we look around we can see the differences in everything that exists. And these differences to us are beautiful. These differences make the world remarkable for us. When we look at nature and its trees, for instance, there are just over 60,000 different types of trees alone on this earth. As we look at these trees not even knowing most of their names, we as a whole enjoy their differences. We travel from various areas in the world to view and enjoy a different setup of nature. Again, we call this beautiful, and we'll say this is a beautiful experience. It's as if nature's beauty cannot be denied by any of us. Even if you are not a nature person, there is some aspect of nature that you can appreciate. At the minimum, you can at least understand why others appreciate nature. For many of us, nature is our truth and can teach us about ourselves. So when we look at the various cultures, and the many different ways that we as humans appear, how is it possible that we are calling each other and ourselves ugly? It's a lie that some of us have bought into, that has been transferred to us from generation to generation. We know it's a lie because again look at how we view nature and all its diversity.

We can get mixed signals about our appearance because we see and hear over and over about how we are different from the mainstream or the media represented beauty that often does not represent us. Because of which you may want to tell yourself that you are not beautiful. Which again would be a lie to yourself, but since you are saying it to yourself, you'll believe it. And if you believe that you are ugly, this will affect your self-worth which will affect everything that you do or want to do in your life.

If you are part of an unfortunate group where your family members have labeled and verbalized you as ugly, this will be a very difficult path for you to endure. Our families, especially our parents have so much influence over us as we are growing up, that right or wrong, whatever they knowingly or unknowingly teach us about ourselves we will be inclined to believe them. As a matter of fact, what your parents believe about themselves, you'll also be inclined to take on as your truth. So if your parents believe that they are ugly and have low self-worth, then most likely their children will have the same diseased view about themselves. And if your parents ever said to you even just once in your life that you are ugly, that experience will hunt you and all your decisions for all the days of your life. Yes, words are that powerful and can be this damaging to us, especially as children. Even so, this diseased experience and thinking can be undone, but it will require discipline on your part. And if you read the other chapters, you already know what you have to do to overcome this. Just say those words "I like myself, I like myself." However, now you can add another word. Do you know what it is? I think you know by now. It's about perspective and changing how you view your experiences, yourself and your world. We lie to ourselves about who we think we are or not, and it's up to us to undo those lies that we believe or tell ourselves. Let's give us new information to offset the lies that we believe. Stop telling yourself the lie that you are ugly because you are not. You can't be ugly. How do I know, again look at nature and all its diversity? We as humans are no different than nature as far as our diversity in the world. A hand full of us is represented as beautiful, but we are all beautiful weather we are represented by the masses or not.

So how do we move toward the truth of knowing and appreciation of our beauty? You look at yourself in the mirror and say those words that others may not say to you. "I am beautiful. I am beautiful. I am beautiful." You say it every day and you keep saying until the day comes when you'll believe it. And that day will come. It's so powerful when you say to yourself and believe that you are beautiful. Even if others by their own ignorance and sometimes, self-hatred speak against you and your beauty, you will have a knowing of your beauty and will be virtually unaffected by them. You'll still feel the sting of their comments or treatment toward you, but this experience won't change the idea of your beauty. When you know that you are beautiful, unconsciously or otherwise you act as such in everything that you do and are a part of in your life. Your interaction with yourself and others is enhanced. I'll tell you a secret. When we meet someone who knows and appreciates their own beauty, do you know what we do? We will also appreciate that person's beauty as they do. It's almost that simple, but you must do the work and have the discipline to teach yourself about your beauty that already exists. It's a matter of do you recognize it or not? Either way, your beauty is there. Like nature, your diversity is your beauty.

Now that you have an understanding of your beauty, and you are on your way to living your life as a diverse beautiful human being, I want to give you a final piece of information so as to give you a possible perspective about those close to you that may verbalize against your beauty. When someone verbalizes against your beauty, and calls you ugly, remember this. Any person that is comparing you and your beauty to themselves and to others is also comparing themselves and their beauty to others as well. What does this mean for the perpetrator? This means they are living a self-fulfilling prophecy. Because they are comparing themselves to you or others to you, they are also comparing themselves to others. And if they are comparing themselves to others, you can believe that they will by their own interpretation of beauty continuously meet others that they will find more beautiful than themselves. You can almost feel sorry for them; because as it turns out that they are silently suffering, pretending that they feel beautiful by attacking your beauty. This will also affect their self-worth, in the same manner that they are attempting to affect your self-worth. But you and I now know better. We are our own beauty and like nature, it makes our worlds so much interesting. Say it again. "I am beautiful. I am beautiful."

GUESS WHAT, YOU ARE ENOUGH

*"Success is liking yourself, liking what you do, and liking how you do it". -**Maya Angelou***

As we move toward our confidence and begin to believe in ourselves, we still may have this thought in the back of our minds, which is are we enough, or worse maybe we are not enough. It's not that we don't have confidence at this point; it's more that we doubt ourselves. I've heard Oprah, Sharon Stone and recently Tony Robbins touch on this subject. I'm guilty of this myself.

When I decided to write my first novel, I wondered did I really have what it takes to write that novel. And yet somehow I completed the novel. I have recently posted the novel **Thou Son's Keeper**, on Amazon. As I mentioned previously I love writing, and because I love it I was able to push myself past those am I good enough feelings. It's the same with writing this book. I roll out of bed at 4 o'clock for most mornings during the work week. Sometimes for a moment, I'll wonder am I'm enough to finish this chapter let alone this book. But because I have a mission, and love what I'm writing about, it seems to get done day after day, chapter after chapter. Even as I read over what I previously wrote in the earlier part of the book, I'm somewhat humbled by my quality of work, I'll then wonder to myself can I continue this level of quality for the remaining chapters. And yet somehow I've been able to accomplish this. As a matter of fact, if there is anything in a chapter that I feel is not of quality or value, I won't use it.

The wondering, if we are enough, is an understandable feeling, but it can delay or even stop us from taking those next steps necessary for moving toward our goals. In some cases, we are worried about failure. We don't want to fail, and we want to do everything in our power not to fail, including delaying and putting off an action that we are interested in taking. I've done this and maybe you have to. An opportunity presents itself, and we hesitate and hesitate and eventually talk ourselves out of it. Then the opportunity has passed us by and we are left with regret for not even trying. That's what I've done anyway. I've stood still and watched those opportunities pass me by. In those moments I didn't think I was enough and I hesitated.

Perfectionism will get in the way as well. We think we have to be perfect to take action. I'm guilty of this. And if we are not prepared to perfection then we won't do it. When I've applied for previous positions, I've tried to learn as many questions as I can of what I think that will be asked. In an interview you're lucky if they get through 20 questions, I'm prepared for over 200 questions. It's exhausting. And if a question is asked that is not on this perfect list of 200, then this could throw me off in the interview. I over prepared because I'm still asking myself am I'm enough. And since I'm wondering, I over prepare to compensate for not being enough.

I've since joined an organization called Toastmasters. We meet every two weeks. What I have learned in this group is that I don't need to be over-prepared anymore. Myself and the other members have learned that we are enough and that we can handle what's in front of us, even if it surprises us. For someone trying to be a perfectionist and over preparing, it saves me a lot of time and stress. I'm not measuring myself against a perfect measurement anymore. I prepare and I go. Sometimes the results are good, other times the results are just ok, but either way I am taking the action, which is what I didn't do before.

We want to be aware of those around us that continuously doubt us and give us the indication directly or indirectly that we are not enough. That type of person can really hurt you. In a situation when you are wondering if you are enough, and then have someone in your corners such as a family member, a friend or boss tell you that you are not enough, then guess what you'll do? You'll do what I've done. You'll hesitate, or worse talk yourself out of even trying. Afterwards, when some time has gone by, you'll regret that decision. You'll even resent yourself and those that had gone against you and led you to believe that you were not enough. That is a horrible place to be in your life and requires your forgiveness for yourself and those whom you trusted that had discouraged you. Even so, the responsibility is still with you. Because we doubted ourselves, not believing that we were enough, we invited and allowed others to doubt us as well.

When making decisions or when trying something new, there is going to be doubt because we are exploring the unknown. That can be really uncomfortable for some of us. Especially for us introverts, which is what I am. It's rare for me to just jump into a decision in regards to my career. I'll weigh the options first. Then I'll decide to move forward with that career decision, such as applying for a promotion or even another job. As I'm doing so, at that time I'm wondering if I'm enough to be able to do the job? Will I be able to handle all that comes my way, such as confrontation or the potential challenges that might come with the job? For me as an introvert, the whole situation can be worrisome. Even so, we just need to be aware that in these situations that we are enough. We're learning to grow, failing and adapting, but we are enough.

You'll see with minorities and sometimes women this idea that they may not be enough. It can be harder for them because sometimes with an unconscious bias they are being treated as so. There are messages that we as minorities and women see daily which you are not enough to make equal pay, you are not enough for equal treatment, you are not enough to contribute on the same level as the rest of us. The list can go on and on. It happens in our schools as well. Sometimes good meaning teachers with an unconscious bias will undervalue a minority student by placing them in less challenging classes. Or you've heard about some of the schools in the urban cities are struggling for the city budget so as to have updated books. This unconsciously tells the kids, the parents, and the world that these minority students are not enough so as to even invest in a proper education. However, it's not just the school system that contributes to this problem. It's the parents as well. I would go as far to say especially the parents. Though an unfair comment, it must be said. We want to blame others for all of our problems, and we could be correct with this assessment. Being that there is a lot at stake, which is our kids, we as parents must be involved with our kid's education process and what they may be going through. This is difficult for parents because they are busy and struggling in their own lives. They may not have an understanding of the impact that a potentially unconscious bias educational system can have on their kids. That doesn't matter. We as parents have to get focused and involved. We have to get the understanding that everything that your child goes through in life and particularly in the educational system will affect their confidence and their idea about themselves as it relates to the question are they enough? When we ask these questions about ourselves, we will use our history and stories throughout our lives as a reference for answering the question are we enough for our present situation? We all have some doubt when making decisions, but some of us carry more than doubt. Some of us carry evidence within our history that time and time again that we may not be enough.

That being said, you are enough. We all are enough. As mentioned in the prior example, the weight of a decision for minorities and women carries so much history and baggage it can be overwhelming at times. And you can feel so alone because we are feeling this weight, but we may not necessarily understand our emotions at that time. We think it may be our lack of confidence, but it's so much more than that, as mentioned before. It's the not knowing that really hurts us. These emotions of confusion and self-doubt are coming to the surface and we do not understand why. This only feeds into our ideal that we are not enough.

The change in our selves is the knowing. When we take the time to know our stories and how our amazing story has brought us to the moment that we are today, then we can process our feelings and thoughts about uncertain situations. Acknowledging your story gives you a foundation of self. This foundation of self you will need as you face the uncertainty of life. This foundation of self is what you'll need as you face the world that may or may not value you. We all experience this from time to time. Even so, your foundation of self is you valuing yourself at all times. This can be a huge responsibility, especially when you encounter a situation where you may be perceived unconsciously as less valuable. Yet as a soldier, you fight for your thoughts about yourself, and you put those thoughts of your value into the world. Your mere presence and your thoughts will contradict a situation of others that don't have the understanding of your value.

A word of caution. This is not about superficial or materialistic proof of your value. Because none of which is your value or is an indication of your value. I've seen people take shortcuts to prove their value, and at the end of the process they have nothing and have accomplished nothing. I've seen people show off their fancy cars and present this as their value. I've seen people with nice clothes and brag about these clothes as if it's their value. I've even seen people hand out phony business cards and present these cards as if this card of a none existence business is their value. When really, they needed none of those superficial or material possessions to explain their value. Just going after possessions we miss the whole idea about our value. And because of which these folks are often lacking the basic foundation of self, which is required for their self-worth. They are merely pretending to have self-worth and trying to convince us of their value and self-worth with their acquired materials. This is not to say that all people with possessions are this way and don't understand their self-worth because this is not even close to being the case. Oprah Winfrey's net worth at the time of this writing is 3.1 billion dollars. Every time she speaks she is showing us her true value, which has nothing to do with her money. This is the point that I'm making to you. Speak your value to the world, think and know your value at all times. As you move through your life we can't help but to stop and take notice of you. There something about you that stopped me to recognize you. You know what it was? I just recognized your value. Sometimes me and Christel will go out in public and people will notice and often smile at us. Other times they will just stare. This happens over and over. We would like to think that they are just noticing our value, the value that we not only have for ourselves but the value that we have for our world. Your value comes from the inside out, not from the outside in. You find or create value within yourself first. This is the foundation for who you are. This foundation will remain intact regardless of your vast material possessions or not. If you attempt to tie your value to your possessions, your value and self-worth will not have a foundation, especially since our possessions or incomes are constantly changing. So when you lose your high-income job, you are down to square one as far as your perceived value of yourself. I've seen it happen. And because you have created this world for yourself of this false value, your self-value goes away with that income.

So you are enough. Your value of who you are is enough. We don't need the material possessions or a high income to prove to ourselves or to our world that we are enough. We are enough regardless of all that. Yes, we may want the materials, and the higher income, but that won't define us and our value. We are enough because we know instinctively that our true value is our existence, and how we view ourselves and the people in our world.

*"Throughout life people will make you mad, disrespect you and treat you bad. Let God deal with the things they do, because hate in your heart will consume you too." – **Will Smith***

Get to know you. We talked earlier about thinking about your stories and how it brought you to today. But what I'm asking you to do is different than your stories. I'm asking you to get to know yourself. This may seem like an odd request, but it's not. As you get to know you, you'll find out why you behave or feel as you do in certain situations. I recently found out something about myself that has given me a new perspective on my life, and as a result has changed my life, and has given me even more confidence. The newfound knowledge about myself gives me, even more of a foundation of who I am and helps me to stay true to myself as others resist and try to present who they think

I am to me. Just this little information that I found out about myself gives me an edge in my comfort in who I am and why I feel and do what I do.

What I found out about myself is that I'm an introvert. This is actually an important piece of information to know about myself. I didn't really find out that I'm an introvert until just a few years ago. But it's not enough to know that I'm an introvert, but how being an introvert affects my life, decisions and my feelings that I felt throughout the day. Some mistakenly misjudge me, assuming that I was insecure or lacking in confidence. And that wasn't the case. The case was that I was more of an introvert, and as an introvert, I am naturally comfortable in certain situations and I'm uncomfortable in other situations. And as I'm learning and researching about what introverts are, and I'm learning there's a whole different spectrum of introverts and their various behaviors. I find that I'm an introvert that functions like an extrovert. Which means like an extrovert I love being around people, but like an introvert being around a lot of people for a period of time will exhaust my energy, and at that point I'll need some alone time to recover.

What's interesting is that I've always been an introvert, my whole life I've been an introvert with the feelings that introverts have. But I didn't understand these feelings and I didn't know the name for these feelings that I had about myself. I knew that I was uncomfortable in certain situations, such as being around a lot of people that I didn't initially know. I just assumed that I was uncomfortable in those situations because of my lack of confidence, but that wasn't the case. This is what I told myself because that's what I believed which is that I had lack of confidence. And when we tell ourselves that we lack confidence, and then we put into action the idea of not having confidence in all the decisions that we make. For me it was not a lack of confidence, it was actually that I was an introvert and I was in uncomfortable situations that most introverts find uncomfortable, which I didn't know about myself then.

Over the years I've come across two important mentors in my life. And at various times they both said something that has stuck with me, and at that time I didn't really have an understanding of the meaning of their statements, but after some time had passed, I was able to tie in their comments to my discovery of being an introvert. And as I think about their comments, to me it's as if they understood me as an introvert. Though others were sometimes saying that I come across as timid, this one executive said to me that I came across as humble. His word to describe me was humble. Timid and humble are two different words and have two different meanings. And though I have an understanding what he meant by the term humble, I didn't really have a true understanding until I tied it into the idea of me being an introvert. As introverts we are often humble, we don't necessarily like attention on ourselves. We like to share the attention with others and focus on others and their value. As I came to understand this definition of being an introvert as it applies to myself, and how I live and interact with others, I now understand I am humble, not timid. People wanted to put labels on me as a timid person, but as I thought about and analyzed my feelings I find that I'm not timid at all. I'm just humble as the executive said. Living a humble life is definitely different than living a timid life. It's about perspective, and if I didn't take the time to understand who I was, I would be living my life as a timid person, because I allowed others to tell me so. I'm a confident person, and I live my life as a confident person. It's my actions as an introvert that is sometimes misunderstood as timid instead of humble. It's not for them to understand, is for me to understand who I am and what I am. And there was a time I bought into this idea of what some people said to me that I was timid, and now I understand as it relates to being an introvert that I'm merely humble. And this little bit of information is empowering to me, because I now have an understanding of my own power, when before I was giving up my power and allowed others to decide who I am.

Another mentor had shared some information with me that was also part of my characteristic of being an introvert. I was sharing with him about my concerns about my voice, and at times I did not project my voice when speaking to a group, and because of which I may come across as not confident. I felt that I had a low voice based on some of the feedback I had received. He surprised me when he told me that I had a powerful voice. He went on to explain that my voice may be lower at times, but he went on to say that there is power and confidence in my voice. He then said that my powerful voice is contained and controlled, and as I'm speaking, there are moments when I release that power in my voice, and he felt that power in the moment that I wanted him to feel it, because I chose at that moment to release the power in my voice when I'm making a point about what I'm saying. In other words, he was telling me that my voice is powerful yet contained until the moment when I decide to release it to the world so as to tell a story or even to make a point to my audience. And I just didn't think of it that way until this mentor had taken that moment to share this information with me. It's important to know this about myself, so when I get the critique, I can defend it to myself first, and if necessary I can defend it to others.

This bit of information about myself as an introvert has changed my perspective on how I look at myself. And how we view ourselves will help us to decide how we will allow for others to treat us. You cannot share your authentic self with the world if you don't know who you are. As you get to know you, you'll find along the way that you can enhance your life and give yourself power. And none of this is about money, a position, a title or income. This is all about you.

The ways of going about to getting to know you are to keep an open mind. Listen to others and their feedback and evaluate it as it relates to you. Don't necessarily take someone's feedback to heart, but initially listen and carefully analyze it. Does the feedback make sense? When people said that I was timid, that feedback did not make sense to me because I didn't feel timid. So there was confusion as I tried to figure this out. I was trying to think how not to come across as timid. But I couldn't relate to this word timid because I didn't feel timid. So I had to figure out why I may have come across as timid. I didn't get those answers right away. It took another couple years before the answer really came to me. But what I finally found is that it's not that I'm timid is that I'm humble.

Take the time to get to know you. You may want to sit quietly and just think. Just think about yourself, about your life, about your situations that you are struggling with. In those moments of quietness ask yourself questions that you want to know about yourself and your life. The answer may not come to you right away, but if you get in this habit of calming yourself and thinking, the answers will eventually come. It's in those moments of being still and quiet that you can often move to understand yourself. As a result, you will be better prepared to present yourself to your world. This is how as a soldier you can fortify yourself. Knowing who you are can make it difficult for others to infiltrate their beliefs and misconceptions of who they think you are onto you. They can try of course, but you with your knowledge can defend their acts with your thoughts or even your words if you choose. This is a power of self, this is your power. Many of us because we don't know ourselves are at the whim of the many opinions of others.

I sometimes find that the challenge for minorities and women is that they get stuck in their knowledge and their perspective of who they think they are as compared with how others can sometimes perceive them. Though progressive, the history has been challenging for both groups. They will take this troubled narration about their groups and pass these stories of hardship and inadequacy down from generation to generation. And we accept those troubled narrations as our truth and avoid expanding out and finding more information about themselves, which could actually contradict this generational recounting. Because this information has been passed down from generations, we become stuck in our perceived limited perspective about who we think that we are in our worlds. And because of which, we pass this restricted idea of who we think that we are down to our families, and then we have another generation of children who are limited by their own thoughts of who they think that they are, and they will present this limited idea of who they think that they are in their own worlds. I've seen parents who come from abusive backgrounds, and then they will become abusive themselves with their families, as if they're saying this is all I know, this is who I am when really there's so much more that they can be and do for their families. We need to take the time to continually expand our knowledge base and our perspective about ourselves so that we can grow into the powerful people that we are meant to be.

So when you take the time to find out who you really are, people won't be able to force themselves on you, with their ideas and perceptions of who they think you are or should be. And this is very important because when you allow others to push their misconceptions of their thinking of who they think you are on to you, this will create a sensation of being trapped. And when you feel trapped by another's will, this can add a sense of hopelessness within yourself. You'll feel that your life does not have value under the weight of another's will. Like the scenario that I mentioned earlier about the elephant and the rope. You have the strength all along to break from the rope; you just have to get into the habit of learning and developing yourself, so that you know your own power of self, so that you can break away from all the ropes that people try to attach to your value and life. This process is a journey and it will take a lifetime. But along the way, you can find out things about yourself that could change and enhance your life which will give you a foundation of self. And again none of this has anything to do with money, a position, and titles. And this is all about you and you knowing your true power, which is the knowledge of self.

PAY ATTENTION TO YOUR WORLD, BECAUSE IT'S TALKING TO YOU

"The key to serenity is trusting that the universe has your back."

– Gabrielle Bernstein

Pay attention to your world because your world is talking to you. Everything around us is communicating with us somehow. I call it signs. Some people are uncomfortable when I talk about my experiences of signs, including my family sometimes. Of course, I talk about it so much that they are used to it now. Because of the discomfort that some people might have with this topic I almost didn't put this subject in the book. Since this is an important part of my life I decided to go ahead and put this in. I'm sharing myself with you, and this is part of my life and would be deceiving to you to do otherwise. If you listen and believe, you'll find that your world is talking to you, if you don't believe then, of course, you'll hear and see nothing.

Either way, it's your life and your choice. I'm not so special that only a few of us will hear or see our worlds talking to us, I'm just open and listening for my signs. Not that you need to be, many are not, and have productive happy lives. With myself though, I need that extra help from life, God or my world. So I look for signs to help me.

This could be your instincts or even a whisper as Oprah has often talked about. I believe it's more though. There are so many miracles around us, including you and who you are, that it doesn't surprise me that our world with all of its miracles seen or unseen is communicating with us. We as humans are very limited in what we can see, hear and can absorb in our brains. There seems to be a whole world within our worlds that we are barely aware of. Pay attention as you make your way through your life and you may be surprised by what you'll find. If you come to a point in your life and you are struggling to make a difficult decision, look around and search for the answer in your environment. If you see something that causes you to pause and to say that's an interesting coincidence. That could be your answer. I understand this may be uncomfortable to some of you, but my intent is to share what I know and how I live. This may change some of your lives of at least knowing that you are not alone in your struggle.

Though I have always worked, my career has often been somewhat of a struggle for me. It's been a journey of growth and learning, but a struggle for me nonetheless. The struggle has not been acquiring and keeping jobs. I've been able to do that pretty easily. The struggle has not been getting along with my peers and bosses. I've got that skill down as well. The struggle for me has been that I've either worked jobs that I didn't like, or I struggled to acquire promotions. The worst jobs that I've had are the ones that I picked for the money, the ones that I was hoping to make a lot of money fast. Well, it never happened that way for me. Whenever I went for the money I was miserable and suffered through the job. And worse, I didn't acquire the money and my personal life suffered. It's interesting though I have struggled in my career, I didn't really struggle in with my family or my personal life. Not that I haven't had challenges, but I've seemed to have been able to overcome those challenges almost effortlessly. As a family, we've been able to maneuver through our challenges. And believe me, we've had many challenges over the years. Yet, with my career, I seem to somehow struggle and go against myself. An action or choice that I have made many times over the years. Part of the reason for my struggles is that I've been working against myself in what I really wanted to do in my career. Over the years I have avoided my inner voice and instead have chased the possible opportunities for money, thinking that this will solve all my problems. The problem for me, not only did I not acquire the money, but I was also miserable in those jobs. This is why I've been adamant in this book when I continually write; it's not just about the money. I've experienced this deception first hand.

So what does this all have to do with our worlds talking to us? I'm getting to that. As I struggled through my career I often wanted to give up. Giving up is really not in my nature. For whatever the reason I don't easily give up on anything. If I do give up, it's only because I've carefully analyzed the situation and finally made the decision that it's not worthwhile for me anymore. It's not that I'm all that tough, though through my stories I found that I have been extremely tough in several situations. It's more instinctive for me. When having a worthwhile goal for me and my family, I can't seem to stop until I reach that damn goal. It's not pride, ego or an obsession. It's more of a knowing that reaching this goal will not only enhance my life but will enhance my family's lives as well. That being the case, with all that is at stake marching forward is the only way to go.

I was encouraged by a supportive mentor to take a career test so as to help guide me in my possible career choice. The results of the test were about 50 pages of data and graphs all of which were supportive to my personality type as related to a possible career choice. The results were an eye-opener for me. The test actually gave me an understanding as to how my personality does play an important part in what career path that I should take for myself. Per the results it was clear that my choice of career should be writing, speaking or some sort of performing or teaching. My whole life I assumed that I could probably do well with any job without regard to my personality and therefore my goal for my career was often to merely go for the money. And this choice was a continued disaster for myself. When I made that decision to just chase the money without consideration of what I really wanted to do, I in the process unknowingly went against myself. The test guided me to get a better understanding of what type of job or career experiences that I needed or was interested in to fulfill myself.

Some time had passed after the results of the test, and I was still wondering about my career choice as related to that test. Then a sign presented itself to me. It was so obvious to me, that I actually took a picture of it. It was so powerful in fact that I knew instinctively without hesitation that what I was seeing was a sign, and was meant for me. When I took the test described above, the results came in a written and data format. The colorful data graphs presented per my answers came in three points that actually created an elongated triangle. While I was pondering the value of this test, I woke up one morning to find a similar triangle with three points on my upper arm. It looked as if it could have been several spider bites. It looked just like the triangle that was presented in the data per the test above. When I saw that triangle on my arm, I knew immediately what it meant to me. It meant get focus and committed to what I really wanted to do with my life, which is writing and teaching. To me, the sign mentioned above was life's way of guiding me and encouraging me to pursue what I really wanted to do. I could have easily chosen to ignore the sign as a coincidence as many would, and just shrug it off. But I knew better. This was a decisive turning point and direction in my life and I was grateful for the message.

There have been other examples of signs or life talking to me. Most are not as dramatic as the example above. The others have come in the form of a coincidence, where I pause and say, that can't be a coincidence. And I believe that it's not. A point to remember is that these signs that you may witness are usually for you only. This means that usually only you will instinctively understand the meaning of that experience. I have shared my moments of a sign with my family or a friend, and they would sometimes cast doubt on that experience. They didn't feel the experience instinctively as I did, and therefore they were not able to interpret those moments as I could. Even so, I continue to look for signs throughout my life. Sometimes in an amazing moment, a sign will instinctively tug at your heart, but you'll have no idea what it means. You'll see or hear something that will catch your attention and cause an instant emotion within yourself. An emotion that is saying, I should take notice of this, but I don't know what this means. At those moments when you are not sure what the sign means, stop for a moment, and think, what were you thinking about just before that sign entered your life. Were you asking yourself a question at that moment, and did that sign answer that question for you. Were you thinking and worried about a problem, and the sign gave you reassurance. Were you thinking about a friend or a family member, and pondering if to call them or not, and then a cell phone ad appeared on your television. Was this a sign for you to call them? Maybe, or maybe not. Call them and see. You won't always be right. But over time you'll get better at this, and you'll trust your feelings more. How I sometimes make my mistakes is when I try to force the meaning of a sign, instead of just relaxing and allowing the meaning to flow through me.

Though I don't see signs daily, I am constantly aware and open to signs that could present themselves throughout my days. As many signs that I have seen over the years, I am still astonished when they show up in my life to give me a message. Not only does the sign show up as images or messages, but they can also show up through people. I have often come across someone that has given me a message at just the time that I needed to hear this message. These encounters felt coincidental, but were they? From the timing of the information that had often been received in those moments, was just my world once again talking to me, and helping me. Open your eyes and ears to your world. Pay attention to what your world is trying to say to you. You'll find as I have that the noiseless voice of your world can give you the reassurance and guidance that you will often need.

VALUE YOUR OWN VOICE

"I think that you find your own way... In the end, it's what feels right to you. Not what your mother told you. Not what some actress told you. Not what anybody else told you but the still, small voice." - **Meryl Streep**

It's important that we value our own voice. To do so is a message not only to ourselves but also to others that we value ourselves and have something to say or contribute. Up to just a few years ago, I have struggled with presenting my voice in my own life. I struggled for a few reasons. But the most important reason was fear. As an introvert, we often rather listen than speak. This is more comfortable for us. Speaking takes energy and drains us. This can be odd because I love speaking to groups and people. But afterwards my energy is depleted, and I will sometimes need to go somewhere quiet to reenergize. We as introverts make the best conversationalist because we listen and are generally interested in who we are talking with. People want to feel valuable and important, and they usually do with their interactions with us introverts.

Fear comes into play for me when there is a confrontation or something of value at stake. When those moments have occurred I have been known to shut down and silence my voice. And doing so have cost me greatly. Those were the moments when I needed and should have spoke up and used my voice, but I made the decision not to out of fear. When you make these kinds of decisions as I have, regret lingers in your spirit. You know in your heart that you made the wrong decision, and the consequences of that decision may affect you for years to come.

I worked for someone who didn't seem to believe or support my goals for advancement within the company. Back then I mistakenly made it clear that I was almost willing to do anything to be advanced in the company. This type of mindset can become an act of desperation, which eventually was the case with myself. Over time if you are not careful it can get to the point that your motive for advancement changes which is what had happened to me. Initially, I wanted to advance because I believed in myself and wanted to make a difference. Over time as I watched my peers get supported and advanced around me, my motive for advancement changed to desperation. My motive changed to not wanting to get left behind or passed over. A mindset of the act of being rejected and passed over. I was miserable in my own pain. Looking back I'm amazed that I made the difficult decision to stay with the company. And the reason that I chose this route is that I understood the benefits of being with the company as far as my personal development and growth. I was able to ignore my pain in failure, so as I could continue to support my family and grow professionally and personally in ways that I could not have been possible if I have left the company. I instead changed my goal from the next company advancement to my personal and professional development. To do this I had to stop and calm myself and to remove myself from the panic and desperation mode that I had put myself. I released myself from the idea of advancement. I ignored the humiliation of others when they approached me about not getting promoted. I started the process of forgiving myself for not being able to achieve this goal when me and my family had sacrificed so much. I began the process of forgiving those that had betrayed and hurt me during my pursuit of advancement. I sat still and absorbed the pain of all. And as I did so I learned some very important lessons about myself and life in general. I somehow found the benefits of these experiences. Through these experiences, I gained the courage to use my voice.

I remember sitting in a manager's office, a manager that was telling me that they supported me in my advancement within the company, but I knew and heard different. Instinctively I knew that this person was not supportive of me, though they were telling me different. I had been in their office several times over the last couple years planning and discussing my possible advancement. I first got a shocking glimpse of this lack of support when I saw a brief smirk on their face as we discussed a plan of action for my career. I felt it in my soul the insincerity of this person and this meeting. But it was a brief moment, and I didn't want to face what I thought I saw. So I continued to have these meetings of insincerity without voicing my concern. I actually was not able to voice my concern for the following reasons. First I was afraid to upset this authority figure which I thought would ruin the chance that I thought I had for an advancement. However, I now realize that I was just fooling myself. I actually had no chance with this person. So it didn't matter what I did or said, this person would not support me. This is why I had to forgive myself. I chose to silence my voice in the hope of getting an advancement. I betrayed myself.

The other reason that I was not able to voice my concern at that time is that I was so upset and disheartened about my situation with this person, that I didn't trust myself to be able to have a conversation with this person without expressing my anger and resentment toward this person. To do so I would have lost my job for sure. That was not an option when I had my family relying on me. So I quieted my voice for a while until I felt I was able to have a direct conversation without the emotional baggage that I had carried with me. This process took time. I had to release the idea of wanting and needing this advancement within this company. I also had to release the idea that I was going to get support from this manager because that wasn't going to happen. I also had to forgive this person for betraying my trust and for using their position of power to undermine my career. More importantly, I had to forgive myself for silencing my voice and not presenting who I am in the hope for advancement. I had to forgive myself for denying myself an opportunity to present my best self for a title, for money, and for approval. None of which I had acquired. It was all for nothing, except for the painful lesson that I learned, which I'm passing on to you in this book.

As an introvert, I would quiet my voice when I was in a public situation that I was humiliated or angry, such as in a meeting. At the time with these emotions of humiliation and anger, I didn't know how to express myself professionally. So I sat still and quiet and did nothing. In those moments I had allowed others to overpower me with their ideas that I did not agree with, with their outbursts that I should not have tolerated and worse my voice was never heard. I was invisible by choice, by not using my voice. The elephant and the chains example again. Because there was so much at stake in many of these conversations, such as deceit, betrayal, and disrespect, that I told myself that I made the decision to quiet myself because professionally, I wasn't sure If I could approach these situations without getting myself fired. I was thinking of my family, and that they relied on me for my income and I didn't want to hurt them and their situation. So I did nothing, for a while until I figured out how to approach the situation without the emotion that I carried with me.

Once I figured out how to approach the situation without the emotional baggage I was finally able to talk to the person who I felt was oppressing me. I had to keep in mind that this person didn't want to help me, which is not the point. The point is that I was able to talk and let my voice be heard, even if this person was not interested in what I had to say. Even if this person was not trustworthy or honest in their response. This act alone gave me peace of mind and released those psychological chains that were on my ankles. Chains that I had allowed to be placed there. I can't necessarily control the other person's response. I didn't know what they were going to say or how they were going to react. But I can control my response and what I choose to say or don't say. It's important to note that I now speak up, and I ask questions. Not just once, but over and over again. Because as I learned if you don't the world will close in on you, and you will feel like a victim. And as you know by now, we are not victims. We are soldiers.

Talking to my boss gave me peace of mind. It is important to note that when I finally talked with my boss about my career and her seeming lack of support of my career, that I was calm, and that I did not have an expectation of the results. In other words, I didn't have to have a certain result in mind. The only expectation that I had was that I would speak and let my voice be heard. How she responded and the results were of no concern to me. The reason why that I took this approach was to lower the stakes of the conversation. If the stakes are too high, then your emotions will rise with the stakes. A conversation with high emotions can be unpredictable. This is when you'll say things that you didn't necessarily mean to say. And because this is your boss, you won't necessarily be able to undo it with an apology. So calm yourself and lower the stakes by not expecting a result.

The worst part is if you don't value and use your voice you can become a target of an oppressor, which is what had happened to me in the example above. I was the target of an oppressor and I allowed it to happen by not speaking up. It's the worse experience of my life, and I did it to myself. It took a few years to get over this mistake, but I'm finally at the point that I have forgiven myself for allowing this to happen and I forgive the oppressor for using their power to target and manipulate me. Forgiveness is an important step in your own healing. If I was not able to forgive myself and the oppressor, the pain of that experience would rob me of my happiness and peace of mind. I would see and experience life through a pain and hurtful lenses from this place of being a victim and of pain. All my experiences would be skewed from this place of pain and hurt. I refuse to live this way. So for the sake of myself, I took the big magical step toward forgiveness. It's a process, but it is a healing process, and it will change your world.

To me, anyone that is in power such as a boss, a parent or a teacher that uses their position of influence to undermine you or to stop you from reaching your goals or dreams is an oppressor. Or worse they convince you that you are not worthy of that dream or goal. I didn't really know that this type of behavior existed until it happened to me. This experience changed my life. So much so that I made a decision to write this book, and to hopefully reach out and help others that may be in a similar situation as I was.

And even worse, you may not find that you have been oppressed until much later. You found that you put them in a position of trust, that you felt that it was working with that individual with their power and that you could trust them, and that the feedback that they were giving you was of trust. So when they convinced you, that you didn't have the capability to accomplish what you wanted as regards to your dreams, or goals, you believed them. And the reason you believed them is that of that position of trust that you felt that you had. But sadly that in my situation I found out that there were alternative motives from this person, which was to undermine myself worth. This is an oppressor. And when the oppressor undermines your worth, it is like the elephant in ropes, you are allowing yourself to have the psychological chains of your mind, and now going forward you don't have the confidence or the belief to go for your dreams and goals. And the thing about dreams and goals is they are intangible, you may or may not yet have the confidence to believe that you can accomplish because you have not done it yet. So when you're working with someone of authority, and power of influence, who has this great experience that you respect, in this relationship that you value, and they tell you that you cannot do it, and they give you their reasons why, it can be the crucial turning point that you decide that you will no longer go for the dream, that you will no longer go for that goal. Or worse that you no longer have what it takes, or no longer have the capability to go for that goal or dream. And that is a tragedy. That is a tragedy for you and that is a tragedy for the world that you live in. It is at that point that you are denying yourself and the world of who you are and what your contribution is supposed to be in this world. And this is why I say there's not a person in this world that can do more harm to another than an oppressor.

Your voice gives us an opportunity to get to know you, and eliminate some speculation about your situation. So often people, in general, will have preconceived ideas about you that are not true. And until you speak up and express yourself, they will continue to believe these untruthful preconceived ideas about you. Even as you use your voice, there are no guarantees. As you get in the habit of speaking up, some folks may continue to have preconceived ideas about you. That's not your concern, for there's nothing you can do about that. You can't necessarily control how people choose to think. However, you don't have to sit in silence suffering. You must continue to speak up, giving yourself permission to allow your voice to be heard. And regardless of the reaction of others, you continue to do this over and over. This is how we change the world, we make our voices heard. Keep in mind that you are not looking for an argument or to win an argument. You are merely expressing yourself with your voice. The more you do this, the better chance you'll have to change the world.

When you speak your voice this is not about being the loudest, it's not about talking the most. I often see people in meetings or in conversations make this mistake, which is to hijack conversations by dominating and not letting others speak or just talking over them. But my point to you is that as an introvert, as women in the workplace, as minorities in the workplace, when you have something to say and you know in your heart that you should say it. It is at those times I'm asking you to say it. When I was in my boss's office, and she was teaching me against myself, I knew at those times that I should have spoken up, and I didn't. And I regret that I did not speak up. So I'm encouraging you, in those moments that your instincts are telling you, something is not right here and I need to speak up, those are the moments and the times when you step up and speak up. And regardless of the outcome, whether they are listening, or not listening, or if they are in agreement with you, or not, or even if they display hostility or not, you can feel good knowing that you're getting into this habit of speaking up and expressing yourself. That you're not silently suffering anymore. Remember this is not an argument. This is merely a discussion without the emotion or an expectation of the results.

When you get into this habit of speaking, you're not only telling yourself that I have value in myself, and I have something to say, that is of value, But you're also telling your world that you believe in yourself and that you believe in your own value. And what happens is people will respond to how we feel about ourselves. So even if they're in disagreement, even if they resist you, they will still move towards valuing you, because they see that you will value yourself. And this is the process of being a soldier and a leader. You set the example of how you want others to treat and value you. You don't let others set the example for you. And like I said earlier, it's not about winning arguments, is not about confrontations, it's about setting an example of the value that you have in yourself, and you do that by speaking and not being silent in situations where your gut is telling you to speak up. And when you value yourself, and I mean truly value you, you will value others. You will value their voices and what they have to say, you will value the disagreements and their conversations, and you will value the differences that we all have. Too often I see people who don't really value themselves, pretending as if they are valuable, and in the process, they hurt others. They devalue others. I know someone who works in a restaurant as a waiter, and often people come to this restaurant bragging about their value, what they do for a living, the money that they claim that they make, and then they will deliberately mistreat the wait staff. And after they mistreat the wait staff they make sure they don't leave a tip for their service. And to me, this is just a sign of a person who really doesn't value themselves. Because when you value yourself, you will also value others. We are all the same as far as our value to this world. We all have a voice. And we can respect and value one another regardless of the different social and economic aspects of our lives because we all have this value. Though we are all on our own path of what we're trying to accomplish and do, and even so, we all have value to our worlds and to one another.

WHAT IS YOUR NICHE

"Change will not come if we wait for some other person or some other time. We are the ones we've been waiting for. We are the change that we seek."-
Barack Obama

What is your niche, what is something that you can do that can make your world a better place? This is something that you chose, or that life chooses for you? As I mentioned before in prior chapters, is that we all have talents, something that we can eventually develop and do better than others. And so often our talents are not developed, but there's something inside of us instinctively that knows that we can develop and be great at that talent, and that this talent can make the world a better place. So in other words your niche is your talent. A talent is not necessarily you being the best at something, though that may be the case for you after a period of time. A talent could be merely something that you enjoy doing, sharing, building and practicing to get better at. And there is joy of presenting that talent to your world, or developing that talent, that you will eventually pass this joy on to others. One of my talents is writing, and for whatever reason I'm able to communicate very well in the written form. I do this better in most cases than communicating verbally. Some of this could be because I'm an introvert, and after a while communicating with folks verbally drains my energy. When I have a choice of communicating with someone verbally or in the written form, I will usually choose the written form. Finding your niche will create stability in your life and fill a void in the world. Whatever you do, as relates to your talent that relates to your niche the world is yearning for. So in other words the world is yearning for you to find out what your talent or niche is, so that you can ease the world of that void. You have a responsibility not only to yourself, but to the people of this world to find your niche and present it to all of us. And we in the world do not care about your obstacles, or how hard or unfair that your life may be at this time. We don't care that you may live in a world that has biases against you. We don't care that you grew up with divorced parents. We don't care that you are born with some sort of handicap, or that somebody had violated you. The world needs you with all your obstacles and experiences to find out who you are as relates to your talents, and present your talents to the world as your niche. That niche is that small opening in the world like a puzzle that is waiting for you to step into that space, and to share with us that talent that you discovered, that only you can present to us. If you don't take the time to find and develop your talent so that you can fill that niche like a puzzle piece, not only will you have this emptiness in your life, but also the world will be denied who you are and will miss the opportunity to experience your talent. You have this great responsibility, and it's not just about you and your wants, it's also about us and what we need from you so that we can experience who you are within your niche, so that we can have a better world and live a better life. And this is not necessarily about being rich or famous, though that could happen for you. We're more than money, were more than fame, our interaction with people will not only affect our lives but will also affect everyone that you interact with, even on a small level with an encounter on a meeting. I once met a person on the bus a few years ago. Though I don't remember this person's name, this person said something to me that affected my life. While on the bus he said in my ear, "Don't ever lose that." Initially, I wasn't sure what I thought he had said, so I asked him to repeat it. And he said. "Don't ever lose that spirit and excitement that you have, that joy that I see in you. Don't let anyone take that away from you." I only met that person once and I never saw him again, but that encouraging moment that he gave me has stayed with me for over 20 years. He was a soldier sharing his gift of encouragement with me. This is the power and responsibility that you have as a soldier. This is how we will change the world this is how you will change your world.

My family once came across an amazing waiter at our favorite restaurant a few years ago. I've had some good waiters over the years and I've even had some great servers over the years, but by far this person was exceptional. This person was the best server that I had ever come across. I still remember him. He was somewhat tall with a thin build, he had a black and white outfit and he carried a white towel over his arm. When he elegantly approached our table, he was nothing short of the ultimate professional. He hadn't said a word yet, and I couldn't help but to take notice and come to the quick conclusion that there is something special here. As the evening went on, he did not disappoint the initial image that I had of him. He seemed to work effortlessly, appearing to have such a controlled fun and confidence in himself as he was serving us and others. As the night went on we noticed that he was also helping the other servers with their customers and teaching them. We were so impressed that I asked him what else did he do besides waiting tables? Often when we meet waiters in restaurants, they are usually in school, or this is their second job. That was not the case with this waiter. He explained to us that he was a server and for that moment that was all he wanted to do. It was his niche and he was damn good at it. The joy that this person had brought to my family on that day is still with me. That's the power that he had with us. That's the power that you have with others. We had been back to that restaurant several times and to our disappointment, we never saw him again. Turns out he was a trainer for this national chain's wait staff, and he was merely passing through when we saw him. This is a prime example of someone with a talent, which is fulfilling a niche that is serving others.

So as you can see this idea of your niche could actually be a simple choice. It would depend on who you are and what would bring you joy, and how you want to share yourself with your world. I've personally read numerous books and listened to just as many tapes about goal setting and trying to figure out how to accomplish what I wanted. The challenge that I had found for myself was that often I tried to force a goal for myself that did not necessarily fit in with my niche. Though I gained experience from attempting these goals, often it was difficult to accomplish these goals if at all. And the reason being is because it was not within my niche, I knew in my heart that the goals that I set for myself was not within my passion of what I really wanted to do or what my heart was telling me to do. So what happened is that I was attempting these goals that were not within my niche, wasn't within my passions or my talents. As far as developing my talents, I found I did not have joy when pursuing these goals. And after a while, you lose steam. What keeps you motivated is when you're working on something that's within your talents, within your niche, within your passion, and then what happens is as you're working towards the goal it becomes play and there's excitement there. This young man that was a waiter, which was his niche and his passion of service to others, turns out he wasn't just a waiter or server there, but he was a leader of the other waiters and servers. He was so good, so passionate, so talented in what he did, that he found a niche within this chain restaurant that had allowed for him to not only to share what he did with the customers, but he shared his service with the other wait staff so as to help them become better at their jobs as well.

I have changed my perspective on setting goals for myself. Now the goals that I have are goals that fit within my niche, within my talents as I'm trying to develop myself, within my passions that I feel that I have. And for me those talents, those passions, are writing, and speaking. And I find because I have set these goals within my talents and my passions, it so much easier to accomplish the goals that I set for myself. I mentioned earlier that I regularly get up at four o'clock in the morning to write. Because this goal is within my niche, I'm able to do it, when actually I did not have this discipline with other goals that I had set for myself that were not within my niche. If the goal was not within my niche I found that often I didn't have the energy or drive to see it through.

You could actually have several talents or niches to fulfill your life. For example look at Magic Johnson the prior basketball star that has long since been retired. When he played basketball this was his niche and he made his mark in the game. Once he had retired as a professional basketball player, he then pursued and developed his talents in business. As a result, he has also found his niche in business and has made an impact on the business community as well.

As I have mentioned before in earlier chapters my wife's talents is she's a problem solver. If you have a problem in your company and you come to her for help, she will solve it. I've seen this time and time again. Not only has she contributed to the companies that she has worked, but she also helped friends and family that were self-employed to solve some of their initial problems. This is her talent to her world therefore her niche. She often says I don't know what I want to do with my life, and yet when I watch her, she is already doing it. She solves challenging problems. I once saw her take on a very large project with the company that she once worked. Several people before her had tried to take on this project and fell short. The company finally presented the project to my wife. She assembled a team and they successfully completed this project. Along the way, there were doubters and resisters. Some resisted and doubter her and her team all the way until the day the project was released. Most of us would have folded or failed in that situation. However, my wife is a problem solver, and because of which, she just kept solving one problem after another until the project was finally released.   She faced every problem and obstacle that came her way and got that project complete. Not that it was easy for her because it was not but she got that project done because in part she is a problem solver, and this was within her niche.

"What counts in life is not the mere fact that we have lived. It is what difference we have made to the lives of others that will determine the significance of the life we lead." - **Nelson Mandela**

We need you. We need you to go after your dreams and make this place a better place for not only yourself but for the rest of us as well. I find it interesting that one of the reasons that I wrote this book is because we need you. This is how important and valuable that you are to the world. From my personal experience, I learned there are a lot of untapped resources in people, and people aren't living up to their full potential. I found from my life and experience that sometimes we are discouraged to live up to our potential. To me this is sad. I particularly see this happening for minorities and women. And worse I've even witnessed minorities and women discouraging and destroying one another. Not only have I seen this, but I've personally experienced these acts throughout my entire life. This is one of the reasons why I wrote this book. I don't want anybody to go through what I've been through. And I don't want you to have that hopeless feeling that I once had, the same hopeless feeling that I know many of you have today. We as minorities, in particular, tend to deceive ourselves about our ill perceived value of our lives. We pretend things are ok when we know in our hearts that nothing with our lives and how we really feel about ourselves is ok. We foolishly attach our value to material things and job titles that won't last. And when these material things go away, or that title is no longer available to us, then our superficial self-worth goes along with that possession or job title. This book is not about the materials of life. Though you will have and enjoy those materials, this book is about you and how wonderful and valuable you really are. That's the lesson that I learned about myself as I too once merely pursued the materials, thinking this is where my value was. Through the grace of God and my wonderful life lessons, though often painful I have learned the most through those experiences from those that have tried to deny and discourage me from a material goal such as a position or money. For a time I felt captured as if I was placed in a box that didn't fit who I was. But what I realized was that I allowed myself to be put in this box of who they thought I was. I clung to this box because I wanted the material trappings that were attached to the box, such as money or a job title. Nothing wrong with wanting such materials unless your self-worth is tied to them as mine was. Once I was able to find value in myself and my experiences, I was able to let go of that box and step into freedom. An odd thing happened to me as I stepped into freedom. I realized that those who tried to place me in this box of who they thought I was or should be, was actually living in a self-inflicted box that they had created for themselves.

You and I are soldiers and not victims. We take responsibility for our lives, and we never look to blame others for how we live. We only look at our amazing circumstances and decide how we are going to march forward. We are continuously thinking and strategizing how can we get better, what do we need to learn at this moment, what lesson is before us that we can grow from, what's our next step, and how do we muster the courage and strength that we know that we already have to take that step. That's how we have to look at ourselves.

We need you to get serious and focused and stop making excuses and stop pretending. As a soldier, it's merely a shift in your mindset, or perspective on how you view and approach your life, as I've discussed in this book. To change the world we are going to need your best self to step up. A pretender and an excuse maker is never the best representation of you.

If we are serious about changing the world, then we are going to need all of us, including you to make this happen. We are not going to change the world by excluding one another or by you sitting out and letting others do the work for you. When you choose to stay on the sidelines and let others do the work, your world will most likely stay the same. The reason for this is the first step for changing the world is changing your world, and this is done by changing your perspective and approach to how you see and experience your world. If you don't make this effort or take this first step, then even as amazing as this world is around you, you will not be able to experience this, because you won't be able to get past your own viewpoint of what you see and experience. It starts with you. It always starts with you. This is the power and influence that you have over your own life. Regardless of what negativity may be going on in your current environment or the painful past that you may have already experienced, the change or shift in the view of this world, your world, must start with you.

As you live your life as a soldier, it can be in the challenging trenches of life, the trenches of your pain, the trenches and the whim of others and their pain and their perspective of their lives. But as a soldier, you have to learn to like and to love herself. You have to learn to continually fight that perspective that others may have of you as they try to put you in a box. You must develop your own perspective of who you know that you are. And this will take some courage, and this will take some effort, but if you do these things you'll find that your life will be amazing. And it will be merely amazing because you shifted your perspective, and you made the effort. Keep in mind as a soldier you will move forward toward your talents, because we need you to go after your dreams and to make a difference in yourself, your community, your family and the world. Understand that you will often be alone or maybe marching alone. The reason why is that people including your family are not going to understand why you have taken the path that you have chosen for yourself. They may not yet have the perception and vision that you now have. It will be up to you as a soldier to set the example with love, and to pave the way for them through your continued actions. Even though you may feel alone at times on your journey, just know that you are not alone. There are many of us that believe in this amazing world and one another and we are making the same courageous choices that you are.

Let's work together to continue to change this amazing world that we exist in. Share this book with your family, friends and those in your circle. When I'm in your area, stop by and see me, and tell me your stories and how you are changing your world. This is how you and I will change our worlds. If you read this book, then realize that you are now a soldier of change and progress. Because you have taken in new information, your perspective is already shifted. At this point, you are a soldier and cannot go back.

With this new found wisdom of yourself and your world, you have to move forward and to use this experience not only in your own life, but you'll need to share with those that you know and care about, so you can change their world as well. Your mission is to carry out your new duties of love and respect for yourself and your world. As a soldier I want you to report to me on how you are performing your duties for yourself, and how your world is changing and how you are impacting others. I want to hear your stories; I want to hear from you.

My arm is across my heart for I salute you with love and respect. I believe in you and know that you will do your part to influence and to change yourself and this wonderful world that we all share and live in. Remember, we need you. Not the pretender that was once you and not the one that has given yourself so many excuses. We need the perfectly flawed you, the one that is real and imperfect, the one who now has the knowing that you are a *Soldier*. And that you have been a *Soldier* all along. *The Soldier is in You*. Always has been, always will be.

If you enjoyed the book, I would greatly appreciate your feedback by rating this book.

Thank you again!

Rod Cole

www.ingramcontent.com/pod-product-compliance
Lightning Source LLC
Chambersburg PA
CBHW060842280326
41934CB00007B/881